BANZAI BANQUETS

Party Dishes that Pack a Punch

Riko Yamawaki

VERTICAL.

Here's a collection of delicious, stylish and eye-catching (that's important!) dishes that will make you want to invite friends and family over for food and drinks. These are all such exciting menu options that I'd really rather keep them secret. With this cookbook, you'll be a master party planner in no time!

contents

Icons for
specialty dishes

Item is recommended
for potlucks.

Item will keep for a
while, so you can
make it in advance.

Item packs a visual
or flavorful punch.

Item can be prepped
the day before so it
only requires a few
moments to finish the
day of.

Guidelines for this book:
● 1 Tbsp = 15 ml; 1 tsp = 5 ml; 1 C = 250 ml
● For soup broth: Unless otherwise specified, use kelp and bonito broth (see p 42).
● The microwave I used is 800W; oven toaster, 1000W. Wattage may vary, so please check food while cooking to ensure proper doneness.

part 1

Cute! Visually Surprising
Menu Items

Here's a collection of dishes that'll make your guests say,
"Wow!" "It looks like it's from a restaurant!" (which always
makes my heart swell with pride) Although regular dishes
could do at parties, naturally you prefer to serve different,
impressive fare. Bring these surprise-packed plates to the
table. Yams and kiwis, pineapple and scallops and other
unexpected, delicious and adorable combinations plus a
lineup of colorful dips will wow your dining companions.

Zucchini Rolls

Keep some skin on so they can see it's zucchini and not a caterpillar (LOL).

Ingredients (serves 4)
1 zucchini
1/2 round Camembert cheese (1 3/4 oz; 50 g)
Salt, to taste

1 Thinly slice zucchini lengthwise with a mandoline, leaving skin on one side. Dust with salt to tenderize.
2 Slice cheese into 2″ logs.
3 Wrap zucchini in spirals around each cheese log.
4 Place rolls on a heat-safe dish. Dust with salt and cook in toaster oven for 4 minutes or until cheese is soft.

Berries Macedonia

A trick to making dishes look tasteful is to use similar colors. Here I've used reddish fruits.

Ingredients (serves 4)
1/2 apple
1/2 pack strawberries
1 pack blueberries
About 30 raspberries (frozen or fresh)
Juice from 1/2 lemon
● Syrup
  1 C cider (unsweetened)
  1 1/2 C white wine
  1 light C raw sugar
  Juice from 1/2 lemon
  3 cloves
  1/3 tsp cinnamon powder
Juniper berries, as needed (about 10)

1 Make the syrup: Add all syrup ingredients (excluding the cider) plus the juniper berries (optional) to a pot and turn on heat. Bring to a boil, then turn off heat. Once cooled, remove cloves and add cider.
2 Peel apple. Chop apple and strawberries into bite-size pieces. Add all fruit to a container and drizzle with lemon juice. Pour in syrup and chill in refrigerator for at least 2 hours.

Watermelon Bowl Salad

Ta-da! Turn a watermelon rind into a serving dish! This increases the excitement exponentially. A very fun salad to eat.

Ingredients (serves 2)
1 small watermelon
1 cucumber
1 pack cherry tomatoes
1/2 stalk celery (towards the root end)
4" *nagaimo* sticky yam (or jicama)
Salt, to taste
● Basil Dressing
  20 leaves basil
  2 Tbsp rice vinegar
  Juice from 1/2 lemon
  1 tsp honey
  2 Tbsp olive oil

1 Slice watermelon in half. Scoop out flesh with a large spoon, remove seeds and chop into bite-size pieces. Cut off bottom ends of rinds to stabilize for use as bowls.
2 Peel cucumber and quarter lengthwise, then slice into wedges. Dust with a pinch of salt.
3 Slice tomatoes in half, then dust with a pinch of salt. Let cucumbers and tomatoes rest, then wipe off any "sweat."
4 Peel celery and *nagaimo* and chop into pieces similar in size to the cucumbers.
5 Make dressing: Mince basil, keeping 2 leaves whole for garnish. Mix remaining dressing ingredients well, then stir in minced basil.
6 Combine fruits and vegetables in a bowl, add dressing and stir to coat. Serve in watermelon rinds. Garnish with basil leaves.

Note 1: Serve extra salad in glasses or other dishes.
Note 2: Place salad in a tupperware container and bring rind dishes separately to be the star of a potluck!

Avocado Gratin

Though simple, this dish whispers "party." Grill up a bunch and arrange on a large platter for a luxe presentation.

Ingredients (serves 4)
2 avocados
4 slices ham
4 chunks cheese (Camembert, Brie, etc.)
Cheddar or Parmesan cheese, as needed
Dash each salt, pepper
Pink peppercorns, to taste

1 Slice avocados in half lengthwise and remove pits. Slice off bottoms to stabilize.
2 Dust surface of avocados with salt and pepper. Add in ham and cheese chunks. Top with Cheddar (or Parmesan) and grill in toaster oven for 5 minutes.
3 Plate and garnish with pink peppercorns.

Bean & Yogurt Salad

Beans in a hill of white. Please your guests with this very stylish and unexpected dish.

Ingredients (serves 4)
1 can beans (red kidney beans, chickpeas, soy beans, etc.)
1 1/4 C (300 g) yogurt (unsweetened, plain)
1/2 tsp salt
Juice from 1/2 lemon
Mayonnaise, to taste
Dill, for garnish

1 Line a strainer with paper towels and add yogurt. Let strain for at least 2 hours.
2 Blanch beans in boiling water to remove canned odor, then drain and dry.
3 Add salt and lemon juice to strained yogurt. Add beans to yogurt and stir to coat. Stir in 1 Tbsp mayonnaise (optional) and garnish with fresh dill.
Note: The trick here is to thoroughly drain yogurt and beans before mixing.

Squid & Egg

The combination of the melty, half-cooked egg yolk and the crunchiness of the squid creates a new food texture experience, doesn't it?!

Ingredients (serves 4)
5 1/4 oz (150 g) sushi-grade squid
2 egg yolks
2 tsp light soy sauce
1 tsp mirin
Seven-spice powder, lime, as needed

1 Thinly slice squid and parboil briefly in 160°F water (should be gently bubbling and too hot to touch).
2 Add water to a pot for poaching and bring to a boil. Add egg yolks to a heat-safe dish and stir in soy sauce and mirin. Immerse dish in boiling water. Stir constantly until thick and resistant but not hardened (there's only moments between "thick" and "hardened" so be careful!).
3 Coat squid with yolks and plate. Top with seven-spice powder and garnish with lime.
Note: Serve over rice for a fuller, entree-like portion.

❶ Dolce Cheese

Just adding an accent increases the drama and creates a grown-up yet cute dessert. This is an excellent choice for an appetizer for a wine party, too.

Ingredients (serves 4)
1 wheel Camembert cheese
4 Tbsp dried fruits (figs, raisins, etc.)
3 Tbsp rum (or wine or liqueur)

1 Finely cut dried fruits with kitchen scissors and soak in rum for at least 2 hours (will keep refrigerated for 2 weeks).
2 Quarter cheese. Top with fruits and rum. Grill in toaster oven for 5 minutes.

Appetizer Quintet

Knock 'em out with an unexpected combination! Using fruit not only makes for a showy dish, it also gives a unique sweet-'n-sour flavor that's sure to leave an impression.

Pineapple & Scallop Carpaccio

Dicing everything to the same size gives this a sophisticated vibe.

Ingredients (serves 4)
6 to 7 slices pineapple
6 sushi-grade scallops
1 tsp lemon or lime juice
1/3 tsp salt
● Sauce
  3 Tbsp white wine
  1 1/3 Tbsp light soy sauce
Dill, for garnish

1 Add sauce ingredients to a pan and bring to a gentle boil, then turn off heat. Let cool.
2 Parboil scallops briefly in 160°F water (should be gently bubbling and too hot to touch).
3 Dice scallops and pineapples into 1/2" cubes and mix together. Stir in lime juice and salt.
4 Plate, dress with sauce and garnish with dill.

Note: The pineapple's enzymes give this a nice, wet texture.

Kiwi, *Nagaimo* & Tuna Tartare

This dish looks a bit Christmas-y.

Ingredients (serves 4)
1 kiwi
3" (7 cm) *nagaimo* sticky yam (or jicama)
7 to 8 slices sushi-grade tuna
Salt, to taste
● Dressing
  1 tsp vinegar
  1 Tbsp soy sauce
  1 Tbsp mirin
Parsley and lemon, as needed

1 Peel kiwi and *nagaimo* and dice into 1/3" cubes along with tuna. Lightly dust kiwi and *nagaimo* with salt.
2 Combine dressing ingredients and coat tuna.
3 In dish, repeat layers of tuna and kiwi/ *nagaimo* mixture. Garnish with parsley and a squeeze of lemon.

Note: You wouldn't normally think to pair kiwi with *nagaimo* but it's a great combo. Try adding them to salads.

❗

Shrimp, Strawberry & Green Peas Cocktail

Shrimp and strawberries? What's this green stuff? The natural colors of the ingredients please your girlish side.

See page 15 for ingredients and instructions.

Summer Spice Cocktail

Just cut up and toss together. It's simple, yet looks complex, which is its appeal. Serve in kitschy glasses for a fun presentation.

Ingredients (serves 4)
1 pack okra
1 nub young ginger
3 *myoga* ginger buds
5 leaves green *shiso* (or mint)
1 avocado
1 handful shaved kelp (*tororo kombu*)
2 tsp lemon juice
4 Tbsp *nihaizu* (see p 43) or ponzu

1 Blanch okra and chop into thin bite-size pieces. Mince both types of ginger. Slice *shiso* leaves in half lengthwise, then finely slice. Remove pit from avocado and dice meat into 1/2" cubes.
2 Add ingredients from step 1 to a bowl. Shred shaved kelp and add to bowl. Drizzle with lemon juice and stir until thickened.
3 Plate and drizzle with *nihaizu*.

Note 1: Try adding well-drained tofu.
Note 2: In order to keep the avocado fresh and green, wait to cut until right before mixing.

Tomato Mango Salad

Just cutting up everything the same size ups the style quotient. Use just lemon juice and salt to keep it crisp and simple.

Ingredients (serves 4)
1 tomato
1 mango
1/2 cucumber
20 cubes cheddar cheese
1 Tbsp lemon juice
1/2 tsp salt

1 Peel cucumber and dice into 1/3" cubes. Dust with a pinch of salt (extra) and let sit for 10 minutes. Squeeze out liquid.
2 Remove seeds from tomato. Peel and remove pit from mango. Dice both into 1/3" cubes.
3 Stir together lemon juice and salt in a bowl. Add in cucumber, tomato, mango and cheese.

Note: Try using other salty cheeses such as Feta or Pecorino.

◼ Heartening Helper Dips

Make these dips ahead of time and they become super handy. These recipes offer new twists on common favorites.

Just Stir♪ Super Simple Sour Cream Siblings

These all share the same base ingredient, yet they all have totally different personalities. Just revealing this secret will impress your guests.

■ Sour Cream & Marmalade

Ingredients
3 Tbsp sour cream
3 heaping Tbsp marmalade
1 tsp lemon juice

1 Set aside some marmalade for garnish. Combine remaining marmalade, sour cream and lemon juice.
2 Plate and top with extra marmalade.

Note: As with all these dips, keep refrigerated until ready to serve.

■ Sour Cream & Coffee

Ingredients
4 Tbsp sour cream
1 heaping Tbsp instant coffee
2 tsp dark brown sugar
1 Tbsp maple syrup

1 Set aside some coffee for garnish. Combine remaining coffee, sour cream and sugar.
2 Stir in maple syrup. Plate and top with extra instant coffee.

■ Sour Cream & Avocado

Ingredients
3 Tbsp sour cream
1/2 avocado
3 oz (80 g) water-packed tuna
1 tsp lemon juice
1/2 tsp salt
Dash black pepper

1 Set aside some avocado for garnish. Peel and remove pit, then mash avocado meat in a bowl. Drain tuna.
2 Add tuna and remaining ingredients to avocado and stir well. Plate and top with extra avocado.

■ Sour Cream & White Miso

Ingredients
4 Tbsp sour cream
3 Tbsp sweet white miso
Tiny rice crackers (*bubu arare*)

> Combine sour cream and miso, plate and top with rice crackers (optional).

Family Specialty Unique Dips

Some have a special something that'll pique your curiosity, and others are predestined flavor combinations.
In any case, some of these dips are dangerous—you won't be able to stop at one bite.

■ My Hummus

Ingredients

1 2/3 C (400 g) canned chickpeas
3 Tbsp white sesame paste (tahini)
20 cashews
1 Tbsp lemon juice
1/2 tsp cumin
2 Tbsp soy milk
1 tsp salt
5 Tbsp olive oil
Zest from 1/2 lemon
Tomato, for garnish

1 Blanch chickpeas to remove canned odor and to soften slightly.
2 Add chickpeas and remaining ingredients (except tomato) to a food processor and blend.
3 Plate. Garnish with sliced tomato.

Note: Try using more soy milk for looser hummus. Add even more and you've made soup! Try using soup stock instead of soy milk.

■ Sake Lees Blue Cheese

Ingredients

1 1/2" x 4" cake sake lees (sake kasu)
3/4 oz (20 g) blue cheese
Pink peppercorns, as needed

1 Bring sake lees and cheese to room temperature. Add both to a heat-safe dish and microwave for 40 seconds. Mix well.
2 Plate and garnish with pink peppercorns.

Note: This goes great with apple slices.

■ Guacamole

Ingredients

1 avocado
1 tomato
1 tsp salt
2 tsp lemon juice
Dill, to taste
Lemon rind, for garnish

1 Peel and remove pit from avocado and mash. Remove stem and seeds from tomato and dice. Combine avocado, tomato, salt, lemon juice and minced dill in a bowl and stir.
2 Plate and top with sliced lemon rind.

Note 1: Try using coriander or basil instead of dill.
Note 2: Make right before serving to keep color from oxidizing.

■ Miso Butter

Ingredients

2 Tbsp barley miso (mugi miso)
1 tsp soy sauce
2 1/2 oz (70 g) salted butter

1 Add miso, soy sauce and butter to a heat-safe dish and microwave for 1 minute. Mix well.
2 Allow to cool for 10 minutes until almost hardened, then stir again. Plate and refrigerate for 30 minutes or until solidified.

Note: Try using this as a baste for roast pork or mixed with rice to make rice balls.

Dress Up Your Table to Stir Up Excitement

Visual appeal is part of the food prep process. If your guests say, "Wow!" when they take their seats, you've succeeded. Here I'll introduce some tricks I relish.

When you want to add chopsticks to a fork/knife setting, wrap the cutlery in craft paper to pull everything together visually.

Place single flowers in individual glasses. Line them up or set at each place setting.

Coordinating color combinations but varying the patterns, e.g. stripes and polka dots, boosts the fun.

Try using orange as a base color. Just addidng a flower on each plate makes the setting otherworldly.

Add ribbons to toothpicks for a cute angle for pintxos.

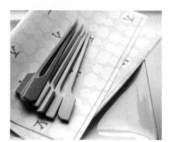

There are all kinds of craft and decorative papers these days. There are seasonal patterns, and they're more subdued than napkins, so I use these often.

I often use seasonal fruits and vegetables instead of flowers for decoration. These are unripe plums.

Here I used a seashell from a craft store to make early-summer napkin rings. Try using twine instead of ribbon to add to the mood.

Don't cute bottle caps work nicely as chopstick rests?

Chopstick rests are key in being tasteful. Little glass objects or tiddlywinks work very well. It's fun to hunt for new objects when on a trip somewhere.

Clothespins are really cute if you look closely! Try using them in a new way. Tie a colorful thread around corks to keep them from rolling away.

This will delight your crafter friends. Spools of thread are adorable.

Grasses, flowers and twigs from your garden give the best sense of the season. Place each one in separate glasses and line up for a beautiful presentation.

These are dogwood buds. These little motifs, presented with dainty nonchalance, add a touch of class.

Just one bloom is all it takes to instantly dress your table for a midsummer fest.

Place flowers in a glass vase on a mat that matches the color. Having everything in one color makes a big impact that's very urban.

I added a quince branch to this bamboo tray which came with Japanese confections. Just one twig exudes an impressive atmosphere.

I use stacking boxes all year round. They prevent things from drying out, and instantly upgrade anything inside.

For New Year's, I use *washi chiyogami* (Japanese decorative paper) instead of placemats to create a festive mood.

These are just wildflowers, but I thought they were pretty so I arranged them in a small sake cup.

Use newspapers (bonus points for foreign-language ones) as a tablecloth when serving meat so your guests can go hog-wild as they eat.

These are the same shape, yet no two patterns are the same. I like how they're not strictly uniform. Asking your guests which they prefer is a great ice-breaker.

Here I used old-fashioned woven *obi* belts. I stuck cosmos to a flower arrangement frog and set it on a small, flat dish.

Which do you want? They're all so exciting. These turn a simple get-together into a festive party.

part 2

Buff It Up! Foundation Recipes
to Enhance Variety in Your Meals

When you invite guests over, do you feel like it's a huge deal?
Like you only have so much in your repertoire and can't invite them over
more than once? I've heard people say this, so I'm introducing these
formidable foundation recipes. With these, you won't run out of ideas
for several (maybe?) years! Purées can be used in cocktails or soups,
jako and pine nuts can be mixed with rice or added to pasta. Of course,
they're also helpful as regular menu items. When you're planning on
having guests that week, prep these basics ahead of time and you'll be
swimming in confidence the day of the festivities.

The vivid green color is enchanting.
Add more soy milk to make soup, or use
in a conversation-piece appetizer.

Puréed Green Peas

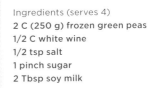

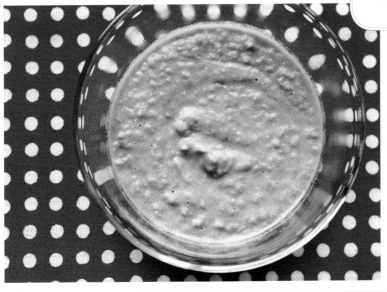

Ingredients (serves 4)
2 C (250 g) frozen green peas
1/2 C white wine
1/2 tsp salt
1 pinch sugar
2 Tbsp soy milk

1 Add frozen green peas to a
pot and place over heat.
2 Once peas have thawed add
white wine. Once bubbling,
add salt, sugar and soy milk.
Heat until just about boiling.
3 Pour mixture into a blender
and blend.

Note: This keeps frozen for 2 weeks
or refrigerated for 3 days.

Variation 1

Pea Suppe

Ingredients (serves 4)
Soy milk (or soup broth or milk) in a
   1:2 ratio to Puréed Green Peas
Pink peppercorns, as needed

> Add Puréed Green Peas and soy
milk to a pot and heat over low,
keeping mixture from boiling. Plate
and garnish with pink peppercorns.

Note: If you want the soup to be even
smoother, strain through a fine mesh strainer.

Variation 2

Shrimp, Strawberry & Peas Cocktail

Ingredients (serves 4)
1 C Puréed Green Peas
8 large shrimp (headless)
8 strawberries
1 Tbsp lemon juice
1 C Sour Cream & Marmalade
   (see p 10)
Parsley, as needed

1 Peel and devein shrimp. Dust
with salt (extra) and rinse. Dust
with starch (extra) to pull off
any dirt, then rinse again.
2 Boil shrimp until red and
opaque. Cut into thirds and
drizzle with lemon juice.
3 Slice strawberries into 4 to 6
equal parts.
4 In glasses, layer strawberries,
Sour Cream & Marmalade, and
shrimp, then repeat. Top with
plenty of Puréed Green Peas.
Garnish with parsley.

Just steep dried fruits in vinegar! Use in place of salad dressing or serve as canapés.

Foundation Recipe

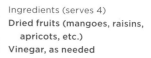

Vinegared Dried Fruits

Ingredients (serves 4)
Dried fruits (mangoes, raisins, apricots, etc.)
Vinegar, as needed

> Place dried fruits in a storage container and add vinegar until fruits are submerged. Let sit for at least half a day.

Note 1: This will keep, covered, for up to 5 days in the refrigerator.
Note 2: If you use dried fruits instead of sugar, they lend a gentle sweetness to dishes.

Variation 1

Mango & Cranberry Salad

Ingredients (serves 4-5)
2/3 C Vinegared Dried Fruits (Here, use 4 slices mango, 20 cranberries and 2/3 C vinegar. Slice mango into bite-size pieces.)
Leafy vegetable (endive, arugula, etc.)
Olive oil, to taste

> Rinse and drain vegetable and add to a bowl. Add Vinegared Dried Fruits (including vinegar) and lightly toss. Try drizzling with olive oil.

Variation 2

Avocado & Bitter Veggie Salad

Ingredients (serves 4-5)

2/3 C Vinegared Dried Fruits (Here, use 3 prunes rinsed in boiling water to cut sweetness, 5 figs and 2/3 C vinegar. Chop all fruit into bite-size pieces.)

1 avocado

1 leaf chicory (or several endive leaves)

2 stalks celery

1 3/4 oz (50 g) walnuts

3 1/2 oz (100 g) cheese (Feta, cream cheese, etc.)

Poached egg

1 Peel and remove pit from avocado. Chop avocado, chicory, celery, walnuts and cheese into bite-size pieces and add to a bowl. Add Vinegared Dried Fruits (including vinegar) and toss well.

2 Plate and top with poached egg (optional), breaking it down as you proceed.

Note: This is delicious on baguette bread or crackers, too.

Variation 3

Dolce Toast

Ingredients (serves 4)

2/3 C Vinegared Dried Fruits (Here, use 5 slices mango, 30 raisins and 2/3 C vinegar. Chop mango into raisin-sized pieces.)

4 (8 if small) sliced bread (crisp)

1 3/4 oz (50 g) cream cheese (or sliced cheese)

Honey or maple syrup, to taste

> Slather bread with cream cheese, top with Vinegared Dried Fruits (lightly whipping off the vinegar) and cook in toaster oven for 2 to 3 minutes. Drizzle with honey, to taste.

This staple gets a lot of appearances at our house. It's perfect as-is for a snack or mixed with rice or pasta.

Foundation
Recipe

Non-Stop *Jako* & Pine Nuts

Ingredients
3 1/2 oz (100 g) *jako* (baby sardines, dried or raw)
1 3/4 oz (50 g) pine nuts
1 3/4 oz (50 g) walnuts
2 Tbsp sesame oil
Pumpkin seeds, goji berries, to taste

1 Place *jako* in a strainer and douse with boiling water to remove odors. Heat sesame oil in a frying pan. Add *jako* and stir-fry for about 5 minutes (longer if using raw *jako*) or until lightly browned and jumping.
2 Stir in pine nuts and walnuts, and if available pumpkin seeds and goji berries, and stir-fry, making sure nothing burns.

Note: This will keep refrigerated for 1 week.

Variation 1

Jako & Pine Nuts on Tofu

Ingredients
1 1/2 C *Jako* & Pine Nuts
2 blocks firm tofu
● Vinegared Soy Sauce
  1 Tbsp soy sauce
  1 Tbsp vinegar

1 Wipe away dampness from tofu with paper towels.
2 Chop tofu into bite-size pieces and top with freshly made *Jako* & Pine Nuts. Drizzle with vinegared soy sauce.

Note: If using premade *Jako* & Pine Nuts, toast lightly in a frying pan before adding to tofu.

Variation 2

Jako & Pine Nuts Pasta

Ingredients (serves 4)
1 C *Jako* & Pine Nuts
7 oz (200 g) pasta (any kind)
   1/2 tsp salt
3 1/2 oz (100 g) bacon
1 can oil-packed sardines
Dash vegetable oil
Lemon, as needed

1 Bring plenty of water to a boil, add salt and cook pasta for 1 minute less than indicated in directions on package.
2 Heat oil in a frying pan and stir-fry minced bacon. Add sardines and break up as you stir-fry. Add *Jako* & Pine Nuts and continue to stir-fry. Add drained pasta to mixture and stir to coat. Drizzle with a squeeze of lemon juice before serving.

Variation 3

Jako & Pine Nuts Rice

Ingredients (serves 4)
Jako & Pine Nuts
Cooked white rice

> Just mix *Jako* & Pine Nuts into freshly cooked rice.

Just whip this up in a food processor. Add this very handy dressing to boiled vegetables for an instant touch of class.

Foundation Recipe

Tofu Walnut Dressing

Ingredients
1/2 block (5 1/4 oz; 150 g) silken tofu
1 oz (30 g) walnuts
2 Tbsp white miso
1 Tbsp white sesame paste (tahini)
2 tsp dark brown sugar
2 tsp light soy sauce
1 tsp mirin
2 Tbsp unsweetened soy milk
1/3 tsp salt

> Blend all ingredients in a food processor until smooth.

Note 1: Add 1 Tbsp vinegar for a Japanese mayo-like dressing. Good for salads.
Note 2: Use up within 2 days.

Variation 1

Japanese-Style Egg Salad Toast

Ingredients (serves 4)
2 Tbsp Tofu Walnut Dressing
2 eggs
1 pinch salt
8 slices baguette bread
Dried plum seasoning
   (*yukari*), to taste

1 Hard-boil eggs (about 12 minutes), then peel.
2 Add Tofu Walnut Dressing, eggs and salt to a bowl and stir with a fork, mashing up eggs.
3 Lightly toast bread and top with egg salad. Top with dried plum seasoning.

On snow peas.

With seasonal produce like figs, muscat grapes and beans.

On boiled broccoli raab garnished with candied kumquat.

Variation 2

Seasonal Vegetables with Tofu Dressing

Simply add Tofu Walnut Dressing to boiled veggies!

● How to boil leafy vegetables

It's actually pretty difficult to boil greens well. The main issue is time, so keep your eyes on the pan as they boil.

● For single bunches

1 Use just the leaves or separate leaves and stems when using *shungiku* or other leafy greens.

2 Boil water in a frying pan or other pan wide enough that the leaves won't overlap too much. Add stems, then 10 seconds later add leaves. Cover, slowly count to 5, then turn off heat. Let sit for 20 seconds, then drain and rinse under cold water.

■ Candied Kumquats

Isn't it unexpected to pair these with vegetables? Try them as pintxos, too. Their natural orange color provides a nice contrast.

Ingredients
20 kumquats
1 light C (180 g) raw sugar
1 1/4 C gin
1 Tbsp Cointreau
1 Tbsp lemon juice
1 spring fresh rosemary
3 dried cloves

1 Rinse kumquats. Soak in water for 30 minutes.

2 Drain kumquats, remove stems and poke several holes in each with a toothpick to prevent them from bursting while cooking.

3 Add kumquats and remaining ingredients to a pot and simmer over low heat for about 30 minutes. Let cool in pot.

This tomato sauce is purely tomato—no oil, garlic or water. It's simple, which makes it easy to incorporate into a variety of cuisines.

Foundation Recipe

Grown-Up Tomato Sauce

Ingredients
4 large tomatoes
1 1/4 C (280 g) diced canned tomatoes (in water)
1 tsp sea salt
1 tsp sugar

1 Peel tomatoes, chop roughly and remove seeds.
2 Drain canned tomatoes.
3 Add both types of tomatoes to a pot and turn heat to medium-low. Once bubbling, reduce heat to low and simmer for about 40 minutes or until reduced by 1/3.
4 Stir in salt and sugar. Simmer for another 20 minutes, then turn off heat.

Note 1: It's ready when the liquid is halved and the sauce is very thick. If you use whole canned tomatoes, mash them as they simmer.
Note 2: This will keep refrigerated for 10 days.

Variation 1

Elegant Pasta & Tomato Sauce

Ingredients (serves 2-4)
1 C Grown-Up Tomato Sauce
5 2/3 oz (160 g) short pasta (penne, etc.)
1 tsp salt
2 1/2 C consommé soup or broth
Coarse black pepper, to taste
Cheese, basil, to taste

1 Heat half of soup broth in a pot and add salt and pasta. Once broth is reduced, add more (warmed) broth, keeping pasta submerged as it cooks. Boil pasta according to package instructions. Turn off heat once al dente.
2 In a ring mold, add tomato sauce, fill center with pasta and dust with pepper. Remove ring mold. Top with cheese and garnish with basil.
Note: Feel free to mix up pasta and sauce before serving

Variation 2

Ribollita

Ingredients (serves 4)
3 Tbsp Grown-Up
　Tomato Sauce
1 zucchini
1/2 carrot
2 Italian or Japanese
　eggplants
1 tomato
1 C canned soy beans
　(or other white bean)
1/2 stale baguette
　bread
1 Tbsp olive oil
2 tsp balsamic vinegar

1 Slice zucchini into 1/4″ rounds. Halve carrot lengthwise and slice thinly. Slice eggplants thinly on the bias. Peel and remove seeds from tomatoes and roughly chop. Douse beans with boiling water to remove canned odor.

2 Heat oil in a frying pan. Add carrots, eggplants, zucchini and tomatoes (in that order) and sauté. Add beans. Once everything is tender, tear up bread and add to pan. Add tomato sauce, cover, and simmer for 10 minutes.

3 Drizzle with vinegar. Turn off heat.

Note 1: This will keep refrigerated for 3 days.
Note 2: "Ribollita" means "reboiled" so this is especially good the next day. Make it a day in advance to let the flavors develop. This goes great with white wine.

Variation 3

Tomato & Hummus Mousse Cocktail

Ingredients (serves 4)
6 Tbsp Grown-Up Tomato
　Sauce
4 Tbsp My Hummus (p 11)
2 Tbsp unsweetened soy milk
1 1/4 C (300 g) yogurt
　(unsweetened, plain)

1 Line a strainer with paper towels and place yogurt inside. Let strain for at least 5 hours.

2 Add soy milk to hummus gradually to soften it up.

3 In glasses, layer yogurt, hummus and tomato sauce.

This is a spicy meat-miso recipe with fermented black bean paste and Sichuan pepper. It's very sturdy and holds its own with rice, noodles, eggs or potatoes.

Foundation Recipe

Meaty Miso

Ingredients

7 oz (200 g) thinly sliced porkloin
3 1/2 oz (100 g) lean ground pork
1 oz (30 g) ginger
1 leek
1 1/3 Tbsp *douchi* (fermented black beans)

1 tsp *doubanjiang*
2 tsp Sichuan pepper
1 Tbsp sesame oil
1 Tbsp *hatcho* (dark) miso
1 Tbsp dark brown sugar
1 Tbsp soy sauce
1 Tbsp mirin
1 Tbsp vinegar

1 Slice porkloin into 1/3" strips and mix into ground pork.

2 Mince ginger, leek and *douchi*.

3 Heat sesame oil in a frying pan. Add *doubanjiang*, *douchi* and pepper and stir-fry over medium-high. Once fragrant, add ginger and leek and stir-fry until evenly heated, making sure nothing burns.

4 Add pork and stir-fry until 80% cooked. Add miso and sugar and stir-fry, keeping from burning. Drizzle with soy sauce, mirin and vinegar and turn off heat.

Note: Speed is key, so prep all seasonings ahead of time—you won't have time to hunt everything down while you're cooking!

Variation 1

One-Bite *Zha Jiang Mian*

Ingredients (serves 4-5)
8 Tbsp Meaty Miso
2 servings *somen* noodles (vermicelli)
1/2 cucumber
Shiso, sesame seeds, as needed

1 Boil noodles according to package directions and massage well under running water.

2 Plate noodles and add Meaty Miso (lightly re-fry if using cold). Top with thinly sliced cucumbers and *shiso* and sesame seeds.

Variation 2

Meaty Miso Rice Balls

Ingredients and instructions

> Shape small rice balls using the Meaty Miso as filler. Wrap in nori seaweed or shiso leaves. Or shape rice into rounds and top with miso like *temari* sushi.

Pork & Green Pepper Lettuce Wraps

Mapo Fried Tofu

Ingredients (serves 4-5)
1 C Meaty Miso
1/2 small boiled bamboo shoot
3 green bell peppers
Dash sesame (or vegetable) oil
2 tsp oyster sauce
8 to 12 leaves lettuce (outer parts)
  or chicory

1 Thinly slice bell peppers and bamboo shoot.
2 Heat oil in a frying pan and stir-fry Meaty Miso. Add in peppers and bamboo shoot.
3 Stir in oyster sauce. Deposit mixture in lettuce leaves.

Ingredients (serves 4-5)
1 C Meaty Miso
2 cakes thick fried tofu (*atsuage*)
1/2 cucumber
1 stalk celery
1 tsp *doubanjiang*
Sesame (or vegetable) oil, as needed
1/2 C Japanese soup broth or sake
2 tsp soy sauce
● Dissolved Starch
  2 tsp potato (or corn) starch
  2 tsp water
Goji berries, as needed

1 Blanch tofu to wick away oil. Dice into 1/2" cubes. Roughly chop cucumber and celery.
2 Heat oil in a frying pan and stir-fry *doubanjiang*. Add Meaty Miso, cucumber and celery and stir-fry. Add tofu and broth. Once boiling, cover and simmer for 5 minutes. Add soy sauce for fragrance. Drizzle in dissolved starch.
3 Plate and garnish with goji berries.

This vegetable relish is a specialty of Yamagata Prefecture. Tomatoes and a snappy, dressing yield a modern, dressed-up version.

Foundation
Recipe

Yamagata Relish Plus

Ingredients (for easy prep)
1 pack okra
1 tomato
2 small Japanese or Italian eggplants
  (*mizu nasu* if available)
1 cucumber
5 leaves *shiso* (or mint)
1 oz (30 g) young ginger (use 1/2 if
  using regular ginger)
1/6 oz (4 g) shaved kelp (*tororo
  kombu*)
● Seasoning
  1 Tbsp vinegar
  1 Tbsp lemon juice
  1 Tbsp light soy sauce
  2/3 tsp sea salt

1 Lightly blanch okra. Remove seeds from tomato. Chop all ingredients (except kelp) as finely as possible. Dust cucumber with salt (extra) and let sit for 10 minutes. Wipe off "sweat."
2 Combine vegetables and seasoning in a bowl and toss. Add in well-shredded kelp and toss well.

Variation 1	Variation 2	Variation 3

Salt-Grilled Mackerel

Ingredients (serves 4)
8 Tbsp Yamagata Relish Plus
4 filets mackerel
  Dash each salt, pepper
  Flour, as needed
Olive oil, as needed

1 Dust mackerel with salt and pepper. Coat skin side with flour. Heat oil in a frying pan and fry both sides until fragrant.
2 Plate. Top with relish and drizzle with olive oil.

Summery Fried Tofu

Ingredients (serves 4)
4 Tbsp Yamagata Relish Plus
2 sheets thin fried tofu (*aburaage*)
Dash sesame oil
Soy sauce, as needed

1 Blanch tofu to wick away oil.
2 Baste tofu with sesame oil and grill both sides for 4 minutes (check after 2 minutes) in toaster oven or broiler until fragrant.
3 Cut tofu into bite-size pieces and plate. Top with relish and drizzle with soy sauce.

Tofu Cocktail

Ingredients (serves 4)
1 C Yamagata Relish Plus
1 block tofu
1 avocado
Soy Sauce Dressing
  2 Tbsp soy sauce
  2 Tbsp lemon juice

1 Dice tofu into 1" cubes. Peel avocado, remove pit and chop into 1" pieces.
2 Plate tofu and avocado. Top with relish and finish with dressing.

Proudly announce they're homemade. Use as-is, on sushi, salad or pintxos. Keep them on hand for unexpected guests.

Foundation Recipe

Basic Sweet Vinegar

Ingredients (for easy prep)
4/5 C (200 ml) vinegar
1/2 C (100 g) sugar (superfine, brown, etc.)
1 Tbsp sake

> Add all ingredients to a pot and heat until sugar melts (don't let it boil). Turn off heat and let cool in pot.

Variation 1

Young Ginger in Sweet Vinegar

Ingredients and Instructions
> Rinse 1 lb (500 g) fresh young ginger and peel any parts that don't seem fresh. Chop into bite-size pieces, dust with salt and let sit for 1 to 2 hours. Squeeze out liquid and pickle in Basic Sweet Vinegar. These will keep refrigerated for about 3 months.

Variation 2

Myoga in Sweet Vinegar

Ingredients and Instructions
> Rinse 1 lb (500 g) *myoga* ginger buds, blanch, then pickle in Basic Sweet Vinegar once cooled. These will keep refrigerated for about 2 weeks.

Variation 3

Potatoes in Sweet Vinegar

Ingredients and Instructions
> Peel 15 small, young potatoes, rinse, cut into 2 to 4 sections and boil for about 10 minutes (keeping some crispness) in plenty of water. Once cooled, pickle in Basic Sweet Vinegar. These are better after pickling for at least 2 days. These will keep refrigerated for about 1 week.

Chop *myoga* and stir into rice along with vinegar sushi-style. Yum! (The garnish here is dill and edible crysanthemum.)

27

column 2

Cheers! Homemade Cocktails

Don't you feel that when you serve something homemade, no matter how modest, it really upgrades your hosting efforts? It's also fun to discuss with your guests how you made something. I love homemade things. Here are 4 easy-to-make, practical cocktail recipes.

Plum Gin

Plum liqueur made with gin is a very grown-up beverage that gets rave reviews.

Ingredients
2 1/4 lb (1 kg) unripe (green) plums (or apricots)
750 ml gin
1 lb (500 g) raw sugar

1 Soak plums for about 30 minutes. Rinse thoroughly and pat dry. Line up on a tray (no piling) and let dry.
2 Boil glass preserving jar or bottle. Rinse, pat dry and wipe with a gin-soaked paper towel to disinfect container and lid.
3 Remove stems from plums with a toothpick or skewer. Poke several holes in each plum.
4 Deposit plums and sugar. Fill with enough gin to cover plums. Seal lid tighly.
5 This is best after 10 months.

Plum Vinegar

This vinegar can be used in all kinds of cuisine. It's very healthy, so try drinking it too, cut with soda or water.

Ingredients
2 1/4 lb (1 kg) yellow plums (or apricots)
1 qt rice vinegar
1 3/4 lb (800 g) raw sugar

1 Prep plums according to steps 1 and 3 of the Plum Gin recipe.
2 Boil glass preserving jar or bottle. Rinse, pat dry and wipe with a vodka-soaked (extra) paper towel to disinfect container and lid.
3 Deposit plums and sugar. Fill with enough vinegar to cover plums. Seal lid tightly.
4 This is best after 5 months.

Note: Try mixing with olive oil to make a dressing or with soy sauce to make plum ponzu. Combine 1/2 C Plum Vinegar, the juice of 1/2 a lemon and 2 Tbsp sugar and heat in a pan to make pickling liquid. Add dark t to soaked plums and simmer to make vinegared plum jam.

Each year when plums are in season, I make plum wine and plum vinegar. For the wine, other than gin you could use *shochu*, vodka or tequila. *Shochu* also works well with brown cane sugar.

Limoncello (photos a, b)

My variation on a recipe
I picked up in Capri. Try it
to cure a hangover.

Ingredients
10 organic lemons
750 ml gin or similar-proof vodka
2 1/2 C (300 g) superfine sugar
1 2/3 C water

1 Rinse lemons and dry. Peel
only the yellow part of the rind.
2 Boil glass preserving jar or
bottle. Dry, add lemon peels
and add enough gin to cover
peels. Let sit at room
temperature for 2 weeks.
3 After 2 weeks, strain out
lemon peels and reserve gin.
Note: At this point the gin should smell
like lemons and be yellow in color.
4 Make syrup: Add sugar and
water to a pan and heat until
sugar melts, then turn off heat.
Let cool.
5 Add gin and syrup back into
container and seal tightly. This
is best after 3 months. If you
keep it in the refrigerator, it'll be
thicker and even more delicious!
Note: The authentic version uses 95 or
above proof alcohol (moonshine?). Try
Limoncello on ice cream, or add lemon
juice and turn into granita (see p 69).

Young Ginger Gin (photo c)

In winter, try mixing this with
hot water. Or add ginger ale
for double ginger ale.

Ingredients
2 1/4 lb (1 kg) fresh young ginger
750 ml gin or white rum
1 lb (500 g) raw sugar
15 juniper berries (dried)

1 Rinse ginger and peel any
parts that don't seem fresh. Cut
into 1/8" slices.
2 Boil glass preserving jar or
bottle. Rinse, pat dry and wipe
with a gin-soaked paper towel
to disinfect container and lid.
3 Deposit ginger, sugar and
juniper berries. Fill with enough
gin to cover ginger. Seal lid
tightly. This is best after 3
months. The gin-soaked ginger
is also delicious, so eat them as
a snack or pintxos.
Note: Add freshly grated ginger,
honey and carbonated water for
double ginger ale (photo d).

Slice up the peeled lemons,
place them in a storage
container and cover with honey
and granulated sugar to to make
sugar preserved lemons. Add
oranges as well for a gentle
citrus flavor. Use these on
yogurt, in tea or steeped in hot
water for mixing with vodka.

part 3

Deluxe Entrées!
Focus on Just One Recipe for Today

Here I collect recipes that make me think, "I might be a genius." But really, all you need is a bit of effort. Hard work is always rewarded, and this line-up is mostly fail-proof. While making any of these, imagine your guests exclaiming with joy as you set the plate down on the table. Coffee-infused pork, awe-inspiring terrine... Each dish has originality. May these dishes leave such an impression that your guests will still be talking about them three years later (LOL) ♪

Bream in Clam Sauce

This whole-fish recipe is high on the awe-inspiring (no?) scale, but all you have to do is bake it! The clam sauce can also be used in other dishes.

Ingredients (serves 4)
1 whole bream (or perch or snapper), scales and innards removed (appx. 12″ long or the maximum your oven permits)
5 sprigs fresh thyme (2 tsp if using dried)
5 sprigs fresh rosemary (1 Tbsp if using dried)
5, 6 stalks green asparagus
Olive oil, as needed
● Clam Sauce
　20 large clams, soaked to remove salt and sand
　2/3 C (150 ml) white wine
　1 Tbsp sea salt
　Coarse black pepper, to taste
　1 Tbsp olive oil
Lemon, as needed

1 Boil 1 1/2 qt water. Slice open bream on both sides. Douse both sides with hot water to remove fishy odor. Stuff openings on sides and belly with thyme and rosemary. Place on a tray, cover with plastic wrap and refrigerate until just before baking.

2 Preheat oven to 400°F (200°C). Line a baking tray with parchment paper. Place bream on top. Wrap asparagus in aluminum foil and place beside bream. Bake for about 30 minutes. The bream is done when it feels puffy when pressed.

3 Make Clam Sauce while the bream is baking: Heat olive oil in a frying pan. Add clams. 30 seconds later, add white wine. Cover and steam for 6 to 7 minutes or until all clams are open. Dust with salt and pepper and turn off heat.

4 Plate bream on a large dish. Coat with hot Clam Sauce. Squeeze lemon on top before serving.

Note: You can make the Clam Sauce ahead of time. Just keep an eye on the bream's progress and reheat the sauce, adding a dash more white wine. This sauce goes great with pasta (spaghetti alle vongole) or over mackerel, too.

Stuff thyme and rosemary into the belly and sides of the fish.

Manhattan-Style Pork

Try asking your guests, "What do you think is the secret ingredient?" Cooking up a nice, thick slab of pork is always a treat.

Ingredients (serves 6)
2 1/4 lb (1 kg) pork loin
6 potatoes
3 small onions (or 6 shallots)
Salt, as needed
● Rubbing Spice
  3 Tbsp instant coffee
  2 tsp paprika
  1 Tbsp coarse salt
  1 tsp coarse black pepper
Dried rosemary, as needed

Load up as many potatoes and onions as you want (and will fit on the tray).

1 Place all Rubbing Spice ingredients in a ziplock back and shake well to mix.

2 Add pork (whole) to the spice bag and coat well. Refrigerate for at least 4 hours (up to 1 day).

3 Leave skin on potatoes but rinse them thoroughly. Halve and boil for 7 to 8 minutes. Slice off tops and bottoms of onions and wrap individually in aluminum foil.

4 Preheat oven to 370°F (190°C). Place pork on a baking sheet and arrange potatoes and onions around edges. Lightly dust potatoes with salt and 2 tsp rosemary.

5 Place baking sheet in oven and bake for 45 to 50 minutes. Use a meat thermometer to gauge doneness (center should be 160°F).

Note: I recommend Gold Blends for the instant coffee!

Boiled Pork with Apple Sauce

This is a new twist on a traditional boiled pork recipe. I reduced the amount of sugar and added apple instead for a mellow flavor.

Ingredients (serves 6)
2 1/4 lb (1 kg) pork belly
1 apple, grated
1 2/3 C (400 ml) Shaoxing rice wine (or sake)
2 nubs ginger
1/3 C packed (70 g) dark brown sugar
1/2 C soy sauce
1/4 C vinegar
Lemon peel, as needed

1 Dice pork into 2″ x 3″ cubes (they will shrink after boiling).
2 Add plenty of water and pork to a deep pan and boil for 20 minutes. Strain and wipe off any rendered fat with a paper towel. Throw out boiling liquid.
3 Add pork, rice wine, apple, pestle-mashed ginger and sugar to the same pan and heat over medium-high. Once boiling, cover with parchment paper. Turn heat to low and simmer for 40 minutes.
4 Add soy sauce and vinegar and simmer for another 30 minutes. Turn off heat and let pork soak up the flavors.
5 Heat again right before serving. Plate and garnish with lemon peel.

Note 1: Use any kind of baking paper to cover.
Note 2: This is even better the day after. If any fat has solidified, remove before reheating.

Saury & Herb Cooked Rice

Cook up some in-season fish for a hearty main dish. Uncover at the table to surprise your guests!

Ingredients (serves 5 to 6)

3 saury (or mackerel or sardines)
  Flour, as needed
2 1/2 C rice
2 1/4 C Japanese soup broth (*dashi*)
2 Tbsp white wine or sake
2 tsp soy sauce
1 pack maitake or shimeji (pioppino)
  mushrooms, roughly minced
1 nub ginger, minced
Dried thyme, rosemary and dill,
  to taste
Salt, to taste
Dash black pepper
1 Tbsp olive oil
Turnip greens, as needed

1 Rinse rice and let drain for 30 minutes. Add rice, broth, wine and soy sauce to a pot and let sit for 30 minutes to 1 hour.

2 Slice off heads of the fish. Remove innards and rinse thoroughly. Pat dry with paper towels. Coat with plenty of salt and let sit for 15 to 20 minutes to remove fishy odor. Pat dry again.

3 Lightly dust both sides of the fish with flour. Heat olive oil in a frying pan. Add herbs. Once fragrant, line up fish in pan and fry. Dust with a pinch of salt and pepper and flip, crisping both sides. Place fish in a strainer to drain off oil.

4 Add maitake, ginger and fish to rice pot from step 1 and heat, uncovered, over high for 5 to 6 minutes. Once boiling, reduce heat to low, cover with lid and simmer for 12 minutes. Add minced turnip greens and steam for an additional 15 minutes.

Note: If you're using a rice cooker, add rice, white wine, soy sauce, broth and remaining ingredients to designated level in cooker and cook as usual.

Bring the finished dish still in the pot to the table to impress your guests, then take back to the kitchen to remove fish bones before serving.

Pâté de Campagne with Dried Fruits and Nuts

"Y-You made this yourself?" It looks tricky, but if you follow these instructions anyone can make this at home, too.

Ingredients (yields 6" x 3" x 2" terrine)
- Meatloaf
  - 4 1/2 oz (130 g) pork loin
  - 1 3/4 oz (50 g) minced lean pork
  - 1/2 tsp Quatre-Épices (or a mixture of nutmeg, allspice and white pepper)
  - 1/2 tsp sea salt
  - Dash black pepper
  - 3/4 oz (20 g) pork fatback
  - 1 1/2 oz (40 g) chicken liver (about 3)
  - 1 Tbsp brandy (or sweet red wine)
  - 1/2 whisked egg
  - 2 tsp brandy (or sweet red wine)

3 Tbsp (30 g) chopped onion
Dried thyme, to taste
Dried rosemary, to taste
Dash each salt, pepper
Vegetable oil, as needed
- Filling
  - 10 nuts (walnuts, pistachios, etc.)
  - Dried fruit (2 figs, 2 prunes, 10 raisins, etc.)
  - 1 Tbsp brandy (or sweet red wine)
- 4 1/2 oz (130 g) thinly sliced ham or bacon (6 to 7 slices)

a Grease and line terrine pan with parchment paper and cover all sides with ham.

b Picture the finished product when sliced open as you add the nut filling (but don't get greedy—too much will make it crumble).

c Use a full bottle or jar or anything else around the house as a weight.

1 Chop dried fruit filling into bite-size pieces and soak in brandy for about 2 hours.

2 Prepare meatloaf: Chop livers into thirds, place in bowl and soak in water for 30 minutes. Discard water. Stir with hands while rinsing to create a convection current, making the livers "swim." After several minutes the streaks of blood should drain out. Discard water, dust with salt (extra) and let sit for 30 minutes. Drain in a strainer and dice into 1/3" cubes. Drizzle with brandy and wrap in plastic wrap and refrigerate for about 1 hour.

Note: This method of draining the blood can be used in all kinds of liver recipes.

3 Dice fatback into 1/3" cubes and boil briefly until edges become slightly translucent. Drain.

4 Chop pork loin into 1/3" pieces and mix with ground pork.

Massage Quatre-Épices, salt and pepper into pork mixture.

5 Heat vegetable oil in a frying pan and sauté chopped onions, adding thyme and rosemary. Once fragrant, add salt and pepper. Turn off heat and let cool.

6 Mix whisked egg and brandy into pork mixture from step 4. Stir in drained livers, fatback and sautéed onions. Cover surface of meat mixture with plastic wrap and refrigerate for at least 1 hour (up to overnight).

7 Preheat oven to 340°F (170°C).

8 Lightly grease terrine pan with olive oil. Line bottom and sides with parchment paper. Line pan with ham (see photo a) and fill with half of meatloaf. Drop pan repeatedly onto counter to remove any air. Add soaked dried fruits and nuts to the center, picturing how you want a slice of

the finished product to appear (see photo b). Add remaining meatloaf mixture on top and remove air again. Fold protruding ham slices over the top. Cover with aluminum foil.

9 Line a baking sheet with a dishcloth (to prevent bottom of pan from burning) and fill with hot water. Place terrine pan on top and bake for 1 hour and 10 minutes.

10 After baking, place weight on top while still hot (see photo c). Cool rapidly in a pan filled with ice water or other refrigerant. Once cooled, place in refrigerator with weight still on top and serve at least a day later.

Note: This will keep refrigerated for 1 week, so make when you have time.

Beef Shank Stewed in Berry Sauce

The berries give this stew visual flair.
Add blue cheese for a meal so sublime it'll cause nosebleeds.

Ingredients (serves 6 to 7)
3 1/3 lb (1.5 kg) beef shank
  Dash each salt, pepper
  3 Tbsp flour
1 1/4 C red wine
1 1/2 Tbsp olive oil
● Fruit Stew
  1 pack strawberries
  7 oz (200 g) frozen blueberries
  1/2 apple
  3 1/2 oz (100 g) frozen raspberries
  7 shallots (or 1 onion)
  2 pats (10 g) butter
  1 Tbsp salt
  2 Tbsp strawberry jam
  2 Tbsp balsamic vinegar
Blue cheese, as needed

1 Dice beef into 2 1/2" cubes. Rub in salt and pepper and lightly dust with flour. Heat olive oil in a frying pan. Add beef and sauté until all sides are browned. Add red wine and deglaze pan. Turn off heat.
2 Add butter to stew pot and melt over low heat. Add strawberries, blueberries and raspberries, reserving some of each for garnish. Add thinly sliced apple and shallots. Stir-fry, coating ingredients in butter. Add ingredients from step 1, plus salt and jam, cover with parchment paper and simmer. Once boiling, cover with lid and reduce heat to medium-low and stew for 1 hour.

3 Add balsamic vinegar. Leave only paper on top and simmer for another 20 minutes. Turn off heat and let cool. (This is best the day after.) Reheat right before serving, plate and garnish with reserved fruits and a dollop of blue cheese.

Note 1: For garnish fruits, soak in lukewarm water or wine to refresh and remove any refrigerator odors.
Note 2: Use any kind of baking paper to cover.

Don't use too much flour. Just a light dusting is all you need.

Spare Ribs with Prunes

The combination of pork, prunes and *hatcho* miso is exceptional! All this needs is a thorough marinating and some time in the oven, so it's perfect for the times when you want to entertain without leaving the action.

Ingredients (serves 6)
6 spare ribs (4" long)
12 dried prunes
1/2 C *hatcho* (dark) miso
2 Tbsp rum (or plum or Shaoxing rice wine)

1 Cover prunes in lukewarm water and soak for about 10 minutes. Drain. Slice into thirds.
2 Combine miso, rum and prunes in a heat-safe dish and microwave for 30 seconds. Stir well.
3 Baste spare ribs with prune sauce, add to a storage container and pour in any remaining sauce. Seal and let sit overnight.
4 Lightly dab marinade off of spare ribs. Bake at 400°F (200°C) for 25 minutes.

Note: If using a broiler, place aluminum foil under and over, cook for 10 minutes, remove foil and broil another 5 minutes.

Make sure to thoroughly baste the spare ribs with the prune sauce.

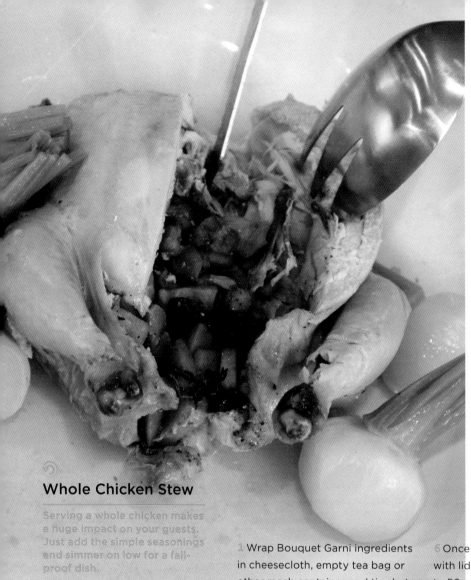

Whole Chicken Stew

Serving a whole chicken makes
a huge impact on your guests.
Just add the simple seasonings
and simmer on low for a fail-
proof dish.

For best results, the top
1/3 of the chicken should
be above the broth.

Ingredients (serves 4 to 5)
1 small whole chicken (about 2 1/2 lbs),
  innards removed
  Dash salt
1 1/4 C white wine
2 C kelp soup broth (p 42) (or water)
4 to 5 turnips, greens attached (1 per
  serving)
1 1/2 tsp sea salt (Guérande, etc.)
● Filling
  1/2 apple or pear
  3 dried prunes, soaked in lukewarm
    water for 1 hour
  3 to 4 large dried figs and apricots,
    soaked in white wine for 1 hour
  3 to 4 sweet chestnuts
● Bouquet Garni
  Cloves, bay leaves, white
    peppercorns, coarse black
    pepper, to taste
  Thyme, sage and tarragon, to taste

1 Wrap Bouquet Garni ingredients
in cheesecloth, empty tea bag or
other mesh container and tie shut.

2 Prepare filling: Dice apple into
1/2" cubes. Halve or third dried
fruits. Halve chestnuts. Add all
these to a bowl.

3 Rinse or wipe out inside of
chicken, starting from the tail end.
Rub with salt.

4 Stuff filling into chicken and seal
shut with a toothpick. If the legs
aren't bound, cross and tie them
shut with string.

5 Place chicken, belly down, in a pot.
Add white wine, broth and Bouquet
Garni, cover with parchment paper
and heat over medium.

Note: Make sure the parchment paper
covers the chicken well enough to keep it
from drying out.

6 Once boiling, add salt and cover
with lid and simmer on low for 45
to 50 minutes.

7 Peel turnips well. Chop off ends
of greens, leaving about 6". Mince
cut off greens and reserve for
Risotto recipe.

8 Add turnips to pot and boil for
about 40 minutes or until
softened. Turn off heat and let
cool.

Note 1: Let cool for 2 to 3 hours (or
overnight) then reheat before serving.
Note 2: Use a pot about 10" in diameter
and 4" deep. Keep the pot size in mind
when buying a chicken.

Risotto

Using several types of rice gives this dish a sophisticated, connoisseur-like quality. Keep the rice on the al dente side to make it seem even more posh (LOL).

Ingredients (serves 5 to 6)
1 1/4 C mixed rice (3/4 C white rice + 1/2 C other types)
Dash black pepper
Parmesan cheese, to taste
Note: Use Italian rice (such as carnaroli) for the white rice, and red, black or wild for the rest. Try spelt or barley, too.

> Add unrinsed rice to broth left over from Whole Chicken Stew and heat over medium-high. After boiling for about 15 minutes, add minced turnip greens left over from Whole Chicken Stew, cover with lid and steam for about 4 or 5 minutes. Finish with black pepper (add salt if necessary) and freshly grated cheese.

Note: Keep the rice just covered with broth (adding more as needed) while cooking for about 20 minutes. This is a quick & wild version!

Kelp Soup Broth

This method is simple—just soak the kelp in water. Keep this on hand in your fridge for when you want to make a batch of miso soup. Try adding this to homemade veggie juice, too. I use this broth in place of water in all kinds of recipes. Try it! This broth adds depth even to curry recipes.

Ingredients and Instructions

> Blot 2 sheets (3" x 4") of kelp with paper towels and steep in 1 qt water for at least 15 hours.

Note: 15 hours is ideal, but the broth can be used after 7 to 8 hours of steeping.

Use Japanese *kombu* kelp, if possible, as it's less slimy than other kinds.

Bonito and Kelp Broth

Don't worry about trying to find top-quality bonito flakes. You can make a large batch of this broth and keep it frozen. Try using other kinds of fish flakes such as tuna or mackerel to cut costs as well.

■ First Broth

Ingredients and Instructions

1 Remove kelp from 1 qt of kelp broth (above) and add 95% of it to a pot and heat on medium. Turn heat to low right before it boils, adding remaining 5% of broth and 1 1/2 oz (40 g) bonito flakes (*kezuri bushi*).

Note: Reserving 5% of the broth and adding later in the process helps regulate the temperature. Once you get used to making this broth, you can start with all the liquid at once.

2 Once it gets near to boiling again turn off heat. Let sit for 1 minute. As bonito flakes begin to sink, strain them out of the broth.

Note: You can leave the bonito in for another 4 or 5 minutes for a stronger flavor at the cost of halving the fragrance. If you do this, don't use the bonito for Second Broth.

■ Second Broth

Ingredients and Instructions

1 Add 2 C water and kelp removed from broth in step 1 of First Broth and heat over medium.

2 Remove kelp right before it boils. Add bonito flakes removed from First Broth. Once it nears the boiling point again, turn off heat. Let sit for 5 to 6 minutes. As bonito flakes begin to sink, strain them out of the broth.

You might think this is a lot of bonito to use for just one recipe, but the key is to not be stingy.

If you buy a sheet of cheesecloth, cut it into a smaller size for easier handling.

Remove the bonito quickly to preserve the fragrance and create an elegant broth (First Broth).

With Broth, Cooking Becomes Easy, Simple and Flavorful

Making broth from scratch can be time- and resource-consuming, but passing on it is a waste! Once you get used to making broth you'll become a fan of its charms. With broth, a recipe becomes so much more delicious, profound and yet simple. Broth is the ultimate sidekick, helping to make cooking easier. Use it to make all kinds of homemade sauces and soup bases. All you need to start is some kelp steeped in water. Start working broth into your life today.

All-Purpose Noodle Sauce

This sauce can be used with vermicelli, udon or even as tempura dipping sauce. Also try it with boiled dishes, fried tofu or stewed vegetables. Mix with olive or sesame oil to create salad dressings. Combine with sesame paste and use to dress veggies. Adjust the strength according to your tastes and add it to all kinds of dishes.

■ Soy Noodle Sauce

Ingredients and Instructions

> Heat 4 Tbsp mirin in a pot. Turn off heat once it boils. Add 3 Tbsp light soy sauce and 1 C broth. Let cool.

■ Salty Noodle Sauce

Ingredients and Instructions

> Stir together 1 C broth, 1 Tbsp sake and 1/2 tsp salt in a pot and heat over medium. Turn off heat once it starts to boil. Let cool.

Note: The saltiness will vary depending on the type of salt used, so please adjust according to your preference.

Try either sauce with noodles, tempura, boiled dishes, or mix with vinegar and pour over veggies.

Others

■ *Shioji Happo*

This marinade helps veggies retain their crispness even after boiling. This is also useful for simple dressed vegetable recipes. Vegetables marinated in broth are yummy even raw.

■ *Nihaizu*

This is a non-sweet mixed vinegar that's very easy to pair with a variety of foods, making it very convenient. Keeping this on hand is like having 100 assistants.

■ *Sanbaizu*

This is a sweeter mixed vinegar. Try mixing with sesame paste to use as veggie dressing. This one is a very versatile player too.

Ingredients and Instructions

> Just combine 1 1/4 C broth with 1/4 tsp salt.

Note: If you want to prep ingredients ahead of time, leafy veggies will keep 1 day, and root veggies 2 days in this marinade, refrigerated. This will help save time the day of.

Ingredients and Instructions

> Just combine 4 Tbsp broth, 1 Tbsp vinegar and 1 Tbsp light soy sauce.

Note: This will keep, refrigerated, for up to 4 days.

Ingredients and Instructions

> Combine 4 Tbsp broth, 2 Tbsp vinegar, 1 Tbsp light soy sauce and 2 Tbsp mirin in a pan and heat over medium. Turn off heat once it starts to simmer. Let cool.

Note: This will keep, refrigerated, for up to 10 days.

Blanch okra, broccoli raab, spinach, chrysanthemum greens, asparagus, new potatoes, carrots, etc. in this broth for a quick side dish.

part 4

Dress Up Your Sides!
Upgrading Your Usual Offerings

Hospitality has a number of forms. With a gathering of good
friends or close family members, your standard side dishes
are plenty valuable. Even the menu items you're used to
making will seem different on a stylishly set table or on new
serving dishes. I made up these recipes by adding a twist to
fairly common ingredients. Once you master these, you can
use them for entertaining or even day to day. Try them with
rice for a bento-style meal, too.

Rum Raisin Pork Rolls

Just roll up rum raisins in finely sliced pork. The cutting method and presentation can be varied for all kinds of displays.

Ingredients (serves 4)
12 slices thinly sliced pork loin
30 raisins
    1 Tbsp rum
Several dried apricots, chopped
3 1/2 oz (100 g) cream cheese
1 tsp lemon juice
Dash each salt, pepper
Vegetable oil, as needed
● Sauce
    2 tsp soy sauce
    1 Tbsp balsamic vinegar
Pink peppercorns and
    rosemary, for garnish

1 Add 2 Tbsp lukewarm water to the rum. Soak raisins and apricots for at least 1 hour.
2 Combine cream cheese, lemon juice and the above in a bowl and stir well.
3 Lay pork slices on a cutting board. Dust with salt and pepper. Spoon 2 tsp of filling from step 2 on the smaller end of a pork slice and roll up towards larger end, to keep filling from spilling. Repeat with remaining pork slices.
4 Heat vegetable oil in a frying pan. Line up pork rolls in pan and fry over medium-low. Flip, making sure all sides are browned. Cover with lid and steam for 2 minutes.
5 Remove pork rolls from pan. Add soy sauce and balsamic vinegar to frying pan and boil for 30 seconds to create sauce. Plate rolls and garnish with pink peppercorns and rosemary.

Try slicing in half and plating with the filling showing. Garnish with pink peppercorns and rosemary.

Goya Burgers

Use the unique shape of goya to create unique burgers. These are tasty even cold—a great choice for bento lunches.

Ingredients (serves 4 to 5)
1 goya (bitter melon)
    Dash salt
● Meat filling
    5 1/4 oz (150 g) ground pork
    5 wood ear mushrooms
    1 Tbsp pine nuts
    1 tsp soy sauce
    2 tsp potato (or corn) starch
    1 pinch salt
Vegetable oil, as needed

1 Halve goya widthwise, remove seeds and pith. Rub with salt. Reconstitute mushrooms in water and slice into 1/2" pieces.
2 Add all meat filling ingredients to a bowl and stir until sticky, pressing out any air bubbles.
3 Tightly pack filling into goya. Slice into 1/2" rings. If there are any gaps between the filling and the goya, spread out the filling to close.
4 Heat vegetable oil in a frying pan and fry goya burgers. Flip once browned on one side. Add 1 Tbsp water, cover with lid and steam for a few minutes on low heat.
Note: Delicious with soy sauce and mustard dressing.

Stuff the goya with meat filling completely, leaving no air pockets.

Sunday-Best Yellowtail Teriyaki

These are two-bite-sized, but depending on how many you plate, this can be a main dish. This cooks up really quickly, so there's no need to keep your guests waiting.

Ingredients (serves 4)
4 filets yellowtail (back side, if possible)
● Sauce
  3 Tbsp soy sauce
  3 Tbsp mirin
Vegetable oil, as needed
Green laver (*aonori*) or sesame seeds, as needed

1 Slice yellowtail filets into thirds (about the thickness of sashimi).
2 Arrange yellowtail in a baking dish. Douse with sauce and let marinate for about 1 hour.

Note: At this stage the fish will keep, refrigerated, for 4 to 5 hours. If you do this, cover fish tightly with plastic wrap and if possible, flip over halfway through.

3 Heat vegetable oil in a frying pan. Fry yellowtail on both sides, taking care not to burn. Plate. Garnish with green laver or sesame seeds.

Note: This 1:1 ratio of soy sauce and mirin is tasty when used with pork or chicken, too.

Yellowtail Dumplings

These fish dumplings are on the large side to make good use of the yellowtail's texture. This soup will make you appreciate yellowtail in a whole new way.

Ingredients (serves 4)
● Dumplings
  7 oz (200 g) sushi-grade yellowtail
  1 tsp salt
  1 tsp soy sauce
  2 tsp potato (or corn) starch
  Dash vegetable oil
● Soup
  2 2/3 C Bonito and Kelp Broth (p 42)
  1 light tsp salt
  2 tsp light soy sauce
  2 tsp mirin
Shaved kelp (*tororo kombu*), to taste

1 Dice yellowtail into 1/4" cubes. (Don't chop too finely!)
2 Add all ingredients for dumplings to a bowl and stir lightly.
3 Heat broth in a pot. Add remaining soup ingredients and check taste.

Note: Reserve some broth to add in if too strong.

4 Shape fish mixture into balls slightly smaller than ping pong balls. Once the soup is at a rolling boil, add fish balls.
5 Add shaved kelp to bowls. Pour in soup dumplings.

High-End No-Mayo Potato Salad

This recipe is light and crisp, allowing the goodness of potatoes to shine. This goes great with meat dishes and surprisingly well with white wine or cold sake.

Ingredients (serves 4 to 5)
4 potatoes
1/2 cucumber
1 ripe avocado
● Dressing
  1 Tbsp olive oil
  1 Tbsp apple cider
    vinegar
1 Tbsp lemon juice
Dash salt
Pink peppercorns, for
  garnish

1 Peel stripes into cucumber lengthwise, chop into slender bite-size pieces, dust with 1 tsp salt, let sit for 15 minutes and squeeze out liquid well. Thoroughly mix oil and vinegar to make dressing.

2 Peel and remove pit from avocado and chop into bite-size pieces.

3 Boil potatoes for 7 to 8 minutes or until a skewer can be easily inserted. Peel. Add avocado, lemon juice and salt and mash while still hot.

4 Add cucumbers to potatoes and douse with dressing. Garnish with pink peppercorns.

Chrysanthemum & Tangerine Salad

A showcase for tangerines. The gentle tartness of Tangerine Ponzu goes great with hot pot dishes.

Ingredients (serves 4)
1 bunch edible chrysanthemum
  (*shungiku*) (leaves only)
● Tangerine Ponzu (for easy prep)
  3 Tbsp soy sauce
  2 Tbsp vinegar
  Juice and pulp of 1 tangerine
  1 Tbsp broth
4" daikon, grated

1 Combine Tangerine Ponzu ingredients in a bowl.

2 Fill a frying pan halfway with water. Bring to a boil. Add chrysanthemum, cover with lid, count to 5 then turn off heat. After 30 seconds remove chrysanthemum from pan and soak in cold water to cool.

3 Squeeze liquid out of daikon and mix into Tangerine Ponzu.

4 Squeeze liquid out of chrysanthemum and dress with Tangerine Ponzu.

Note: This is even more delicious if, at the end of step 2, you marinate the chrysanthemum in *Shioji Happo* (p 43) for 20 minutes or so.

Tipsy Pork

This little piggy must have gotten tipsy. Pork, gently boiled in sake lees. Turn the boiling liquid into broth for soup or porridge!

Ingredients (serves 4)
1 lb (500 g) pork loin
1 leek
2 nubs ginger
7 oz (200 g) sake lees (*sake kasu*)
2 tsp salt
3" x 4" piece of dried kelp
● Sauce
 ⎸ 1 Tbsp boiling liquid from pork
 ⎸ 1 Tbsp soy sauce
Mustard, as needed

1 Slice leek into 2" pieces on the bias. Cut ginger into thirds and mash.

2 If sliced, tie pork together with string. Add to a pot enough water to cover pork (about 1 qt), kelp, then pork, crumbled sake lees, leeks, ginger and salt. Heat on high.

3 Once boiling, reduce heat to medium and boil for 40 minutes. The pork is done once no red liquid runs

out after a skewer is inserted. Turn off heat. Let cool.

4 Combine boiling liquid and soy sauce to make sauce. Slice pork into bite-size pieces. Plate, drizzle with sauce and place leeks and mustard to the side.

Note 1: Run bean sprouts through the boiling liquid for a tasty side veggie.
Note 2: Make soup by adding 1 Tbsp light soy sauce to 2 1/2 C boiling liquid and enoki or other mushrooms and green onions to taste.

Onion Soup

This recipe takes time, but not much effort. You don't need to sauté the onions, so you don't even need oil. This is great for everyday meals.

Ingredients (serves 2)
1 large onion
1 2/3 C broth
Salt and pepper, to taste
Swiss or Parmesan cheese, as needed
Pink peppercorns, as needed

1 Leave skin on onion. Chop off 1/2" from top and bottom. Sprinkle a pinch of salt on top and wrap tightly with aluminum foil.

2 Preheat oven to 400°F (200°C). Bake onion for 50 minutes (40 minutes if using young onions). It's done once the outside gives when touched.

3 Add broth and salt to a pot. Add onion juices inside aluminum foil from baking as well as peeled onion.

4 Heat, adding pepper. Add cheese and melt. Plate and garnish with pink peppercorns.

Note: This goes great with toasted bread.

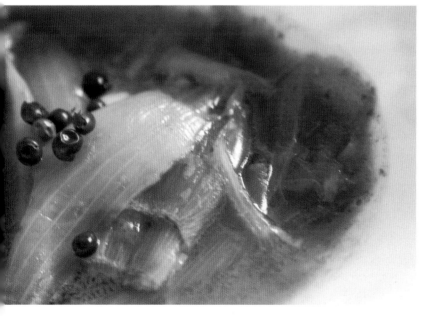

Fried Tofu Rolls

This dish will make your guests think you're an expert in the kitchen. Keep these marinating in the fridge, and time will make them tasty. Wonderfully comforting.

Ingredients (serves 2)
7 oz (200 g) ground chicken breast
1/2 block firm tofu (5 1/4 oz)
2 sheets thin fried tofu (*aburaage*)
1/2 carrot
3 snap peas or string beans
1 tsp light soy sauce
1 tsp mirin
Dash vegetable oil
● Boiling liquid
  1 1/4 C broth
  1 tsp mirin
  2 tsp light soy sauce
  1/2 tsp salt

1 Wrap tofu in paper towels and let sit in a strainer for 15 minutes to drain.
2 Douse thin fried tofu with hot water to remove oil. Slice off 3 sides to open. Reserve sliced off ends of tofu for later use.
3 Heat vegetable oil in a frying pan. Add julienned carrot and snap peas and stir-fry. Add soy sauce and mirin and stir to coat. Let cool.
4 Add chicken, drained tofu, fried tofu ends and vegetables from step 3 to a bowl and stir.
5 Add filling from step 4 evenly on both fried tofu sheets and roll up like a sushi roll. Stick with a toothpick to keep from unrolling.
6 Add boiling liquid ingredients to a pot. Add tofu rolls, toothpick ends down, to pot. Cover with aluminum foil, boil for 10 minutes, flip, and boil for another 10 minutes. Turn off heat and let cool.

Thinly slice off 3 ends of both fried tofu sheets. Open sheets gently to prevent tearing.

Store in refrigerator still in the boiling liquid and let the flavors seep in. These are best starting the day after they're made and will keep 3 to 4 days refrigerated.

Little Snacks You Can (No Doubt) Whip Up with What You Have On Hand

Unexpected guests! Instead of fretting, why not put together one of these?

Potato Miso Gratin

This golden combo is fail-proof and will please just about anyone. Huff and puff as you gobble it down hot.

Ingredients (yields one 4" x 8" dish)
3 potatoes
1 1/2 Tbsp barley miso (*mugi miso*)
1/2 C Parmesan or other meltable cheese

1 Boil potatoes for 7 to 8 minutes or until a skewer can be easily inserted. Peel, lightly mash and place on a heat-safe dish.
2 Dot potatoes with miso and cover with cheese.
3 Grill in toaster oven or broiler for 7 minutes or until cheese is melted and miso is browned.

Potato Galette

Crunch your knife into this simple dish as they watch to heighten their anticipation. Serve with ketchup and watch them smile.

Ingredients (yields two 6" rounds)
2 potatoes
1 Tbsp flour
1 Tbsp milk
Parmesan cheese, as needed
1 Tbsp olive oil
Ketchup, to taste

1 Julienne potatoes using a mandoline. Stir flour and milk into potatoes.
2 Heat olive oil in a frying pan. Spread half of potato mixture into a round in the pan. Fry for 3 minutes, flip, dust with Parmesan cheese and fry for another 5 minutes. Repeat with remaining potato mixture.
3 Plate. Top with ketchup.

Ginger-Boiled Sardines

This only takes 5 minutes to prepare, but it'll have your guests wondering if you're a brilliant Japanese chef in disguise.

Ingredients (serves 3 to 4)
12 oil-packed sardines
2 nubs ginger
1 Tbsp sake
2 tsp soy sauce
2 tsp mirin
Seasonal greens, as needed

1 Lay sardines on a paper towel. Layer another paper towel on top and gently wipe off excess oil.
2 Grate half of ginger and julienne other half.
3 Heat sake in a small pan over medium. Once gently boiling add sardines and grated ginger. Once the liquid has started to boil down add soy sauce, mirin, julienned ginger and boil for 1 minute, stirring to coat. It's ready once most of the liquid has boiled off.

4 Plate. Serve with blanched seasonal greens.

Note: Serve on a bed of rice along with scrambled eggs for a wonderful donburi.

Anchovy & Apple Salad

Just combine tart apples with cream cheese for flavor and mix with anchovies.

Ingredients (for easy prep)
1 1/2 oz (40 g) anchovies (canned or jarred)
1/4 C white wine
1 apple
1 light C walnuts
1 1/2 oz (40 g) cream cheese
1 tsp coarse black pepper
2 tsp olive oil
2 tsp lemon juice
Lemon peel, for garnish

1 Wrap anchovies in paper towels to remove excess oil. Marinate in white wine for 20 to 30 minutes. Drain well and chop into 1/2" pieces.
2 Chop walnuts into bite-size pieces and dry-roast in a frying pan. Dice cream cheese into 1/2" cubes. Peel apple, slice into eighths then into thin wedges.
3 Combine ingredients from steps 1 and 2, pepper, olive oil and lemon juice. Plate and garnish with lemon peel.

Sake Banana Toast

Sake lees and bananas—actually wonderful together. Guaranteed to speed up intake of champagne, white wine or chilled sake...

Ingredients (for easy prep)
4 slices baguette or rye bread
2 fully ripe bananas
2 oz (60 g) sake lees (*sake kasu*)
1 Tbsp unsweetened soy milk (or milk)
Maple syrup, to taste

1 Mash 1 banana into paste. Thinly slice other banana.

2 Bring sake lees back to room temperature and reconstitute in soy milk (you can microwave it for 30 seconds). Stir in mashed banana.

3 Spread banana mixture from step 2 over bread and top with banana slices. Grill for 2 minutes in a toaster oven or broiler. Drizzle with maple syrup before serving.

Note: This is also great on crackers!

Cucumber, Grapefruit & Celery Salad

This is an oil-free, snappy salad with bittersweet, tangy grapefruit.

Ingredients (serves 4)
1 cucumber
1 grapefruit (or equivalent of oranges or tangerines)
1 stalk celery
1 3/4 oz (50 g) young ginger
2/3 tsp salt
1/2 C *nihaizu* (p 43)
Fresh cilantro or parsley, ground sesame seeds, as needed

1 Slice ends off cucumber and cut into thirds. Use a rolling pin and smash into 1" pieces. Peel fibers off of celery and snap into 1" pieces. Julienne ginger. Peel grapefruit and scoop out flesh.

2 Add cucumbers, celery and ginger to a bowl, dust with salt. Mix well and let sit for 30 minutes. Drain "sweated" liquid thoroughly.

3 Add ingredients from step 2 and shredded grapefruit to a flat dish. Drizzle with *nihaizu*. Refrigerate for 1 hour to let soak its taste. Chop cilantro into 1/2" pieces and mix into salad before plating. Dust with ground sesame seeds.

Note: It's important to drain all the liquid out of the cucumber, celery and ginger.

3 Pintxos

Charm your guests with arresting combinations of these easy finger foods.

■ Lemon, Potato & Anchovy

Ingredients (4 pieces)
Organic lemon, as needed
1 Tbsp honey
1/2 potato
2 anchovies

1 Slice four 1/10" rounds of unpeeled lemon. Drizzle with honey.
2 Boil potato for 7 to 8 minutes or until a skewer can be easily inserted. Quarter.
3 Wipe off excess oil from anchovies with paper towels. Halve widthwise.
4 Fold individual lemon slices around anchovy pieces and skewer with a toothpick. Top ends of toothpicks with potato pieces.

■ Beans & *Tsukudani*

Ingredients (4 pieces)
4 sweet boiled beans
Tsukudani kelp, asparagus or other vegetable, as needed

> Skewer 1 bean and a few pieces of *tsukudani* on a toothpick. Repeat with remaining servings.

■ Figs & Blue Cheese

Ingredients (4 pieces)
2 large dried figs
Bourbon, red wine or rum, as needed
Blue cheese, as needed

1 Soak figs in liquor overnight.
2 Slice figs in half. Skewer 1/2 fig and bite-sized cut of blue cheese on a toothpick. Repeat with remaining servings.

part 5

Rice and Noodle Clinchers: Adding a Little Extra Ingenuity Leaves an Impression

I usually serve rice or noodle dishes towards the end of the party. It not only helps balance out the previous courses but is also another chance to give your guests a little ★ surprise. Depending on the timing, some of these can be main dishes, and others make great options for potluck dinners. I chose recipes that will please any guest, whether they've been imbibing or not. Try making these for yourself, too. Pick according to who's coming over for dinner and what their preferences are.

Salsify Rice

Since the salsify is fried and steamed beforehand, its fragrance is more pronounced when cooked into the rice. Its subdued color makes for a sleek impression.

Ingredients (serves 4 to 5)
- 1 stalk salsify
  (burdock root; *gobo*)
  1/2 tsp sake
  1 tsp salt
  Dash vegetable oil
- 1 2/3 C rice
  1 2/3 C Kelp Soup Broth
  (p 42)
  2 Tbsp sake
  1/2 tsp salt

1 Peel salsify and shave thinly (it helps to carve a cross shape into the middle to start). Soak in water. Drain.

2 Heat oil in a pan and add salsify. Stir-fry for 30 seconds to cook off moisture. Add sake and salt, cover with lid and steam for 30 seconds. Turn off heat.

3 Rinse rice and add to a pot. Add broth and let sit for 1 hour. Add salsify, sake and salt. Leave uncovered and heat over medium-high. Once gently boiling, reduce heat to low, cover with lid and cook for 11 to 12 minutes. Turn off heat and let steam for 10 minutes.

Note 1: If using a rice cooker, combine 1 1/2 C rice, 2 light Tbsp sake, 1/2 tsp salt, 1 1/2 C broth, salsify from step 2 and cook as usual.
Note 2: Try adding finely chopped chicken or ham to the salsify when you stir-fry it.

Carrots Only! Rice

Limiting yourself to just one addition to the rice gives a unique feel. The orange color of the carrots is so pretty!

Ingredients (serves 4 to 5)
- 1 1/2 carrots
  1 tsp salt
  1 Tbsp ground
    sesame seeds
  1 tsp light soy sauce
  Dash vegetable oil
- 1 2/3 C rice
  1 2/3 C Kelp Soup Broth
  (p 42)
  2 tsp mirin
  2 tsp light soy sauce

1 Peel carrots. Finely chop 1 carrot. Grate remaining 1/2 carrot, place in a fine mesh strainer and lightly press out liquid.

2 Heat oil in a frying pan. Stir-fry chopped carrots to cook off moisture. Add salt and sesame seeds. Pour in soy sauce once moisture is reduced. Turn off heat.

3 Add rinsed rice and broth to a pot and let sit for 1 hour. Add cooked carrots, grated carrots, mirin and soy sauce. Leave uncovered and heat over medium-high. Once boiling, reduce heat to low, cover with lid and cook for 11 to 12 minutes. Turn off heat and let steam for 10 minutes.

Note 1: If using a rice cooker, combine 1 1/2 C rice, 2 light tsp each mirin and light soy sauce, 1 1/2 C broth, carrots from steps 1 and 2 and cook as usual.
Note 2: If you don't have kelp broth, add dried kelp when cooking the rice.

Marinated Tuna & Avocado *Chirashi*

This hand-mixed sushi dish is extravagant enough to be a main course. Serve in a large sushi tray for a powerful presentation.

Ingredients (serves 4 to 5)
4 1/2 C cooked rice
   1/4 C (60 ml) sushi vinegar*
20 slices tuna sashimi
   2 Tbsp soy sauce
   2 Tbsp mirin
1 to 1 1/2 ripe avocado
1 bunch broccoli raab
Roasted white sesame seeds, as needed

1 Slice tuna sashimi pieces in half. Combine soy sauce and mirin and marinate tuna for 30 to 40 minutes in the refrigerator.

2 Blanch broccoli raab briefly then plunge into ice water to preserve color. Shred into bite-size pieces. Peel and remove pit from avocado and chop flesh into bite-size pieces.

3 Stir sushi vinegar into freshly steamed rice. Let cool slightly. Remove tuna from marinade and add to rice along with broccoli raab and avocado. Sprinkle with sesame seeds.

Note: Stir vinegar into rice with long chopsticks or wooden spatula with a cutting motion.

*Sushi Vinegar
Ingredients and Instructions
(yields about 1 C)
Combine 1 C vinegar, 2/3 C sugar, 1 2/3 Tbsp salt in a pot and heat over low. Turn off heat once sugar melts. Don't let it boil as that will burn off the vinegar's flavor.
▶ Useful ratio to know: In general, it's 1/4 C sushi vinegar per 4 1/2 C (or 1 1/2 C uncooked) rice for sushi rice.

Smoked Salmon, Black Pepper & Lemon Sushi

Smoked salmon has a lovely coral color and is very easy to work with. Bring this to a potluck dinner and become the life of the party!

Ingredients (yields 8" x 3" x 2" block)
4 1/2 C rice, freshly cooked
15 pieces smoked salmon
2 Tbsp white wine or sake
1/4 C (60 ml) Lemon Sushi Vinegar*
1 organic lemon rind, finely chopped
1/4 tsp coarse black pepper
Lemon rind and fresh dill, for garnish

1 Spread out 12 pieces of smoked salmon and drizzle with white wine (A). Finely slice remaining 3 pieces of smoked salmon and drizzle with 1 Tbsp Lemon Sushi Vinegar (B).

2 Spread cooked rice in a large baking dish or sushi pail and stir in remaining Lemon Sushi Vinegar. Stir in chopped lemon rind and pepper.

Note: Use long chopsticks and stir in gradually with chopping motions.

3 Pick a rectangular container (If wooden, first let sit in water). Lay salmon A inside bottom of container (if there is excess salmon, slice and add to salmon B). Layer 1/2 of seasoned rice on top, then spread salmon B along rice. Top with remaining seasoned rice and press firmly. Let sit for 1 hour (in a cool place if the weather is warm).

4 Flip container over and remove sushi. Garnish with lemon rind and dill. Slice into sushi-size pieces, wetting knife between cuts.

Note: Lay salmon A on plastic wrap, top with salmon B mixed into seasoned rice and twist up and squeeze with a kitchen cloth to form round *temari* sushi.

*Lemon Sushi Vinegar
Ingredients and Instructions
(yields a little over 1 C)
Combine 2/3 C vinegar, 2/3 C sugar, 1 2/3 Tbsp salt in a pot and heat over low. Turn off heat once sugar melts.
▶ Use this as a marinade for salmon or mixed with oil to make salad dressing.

Dried Mackerel & Ginger Rice

This dish is simple—just mix grilled, dried mackerel and ginger into rice. Knowing how to make ginger rice should prove convenient.

Ingredients (serves 4 to 5)
● Ginger Rice
  1 2/3 C rice
  1 2/3 C water
  2 Tbsp sake
  1 heaping tsp salt
  1 1/2 oz ginger
  1 piece dried kelp (2" x 3")
1 filet (appx. 8") dried or cured
  mackerel
  1 tsp soy sauce
1 Tbsp chopped fresh dill (or 1 tsp
  dried dill)

1 Make Ginger Rice: Mince ginger. Rinse rice and add to pot along with water and sake. Let sit for 1 hour. Add salt, ginger and kelp. Leave uncovered and heat over medium-high. Once boiling, reduce heat to low. Cover and cook for 11 to 12 minutes. Turn off heat and let steam for 10 minutes.

2 Grill mackerel. Remove bones. Shred meat by hand and drizzle with soy sauce.

3 Thoroughly mix mackerel and dill into freshly cooked rice.

Note: If using a rice cooker, combine 1 1/2 C rice, 2 Tbsp sake, 1 tsp salt, 1 1/2 C broth, ginger and kelp and cook as usual.

Black Pepper Short Pasta

This is almost too simple which is why it's so refreshing. It's a popular dish in Rome and thereabouts. Great for when you're in a real hurry.

Ingredients (serves 2 to 4)
5 1/2 oz (160 g) short pasta (fusilli, penne, etc.)
2 tsp salt
2 1/2 C chicken broth
1 Tbsp coarse black pepper
3 Tbsp grated cheese

1 Add pasta and salt to a pot. Add warmed broth to pan until pasta is covered. Heat over medium, adding broth as it cooks off, making sure pasta stays submerged. Check cooking time against package directions and turn off heat once pasta is al dente.

2 Add pepper and cheese to a bowl. Drain pasta and add, mixing well.

Note: Keeping short pasta always just submerged as it boils is key to making it delicious.

Cold *Shabu* Pork & Goya Vermicelli

Boil the goya and pasta in the same liquid used for the pork to add richness to this chilled pasta dish.

Ingredients (serves 4)
4 servings vermicelli
7 oz (300 g) pork loin, thinly sliced
1/2 goya (bitter melon)
3" daikon, grated
Shiso (or parsley), as needed
Yuzu kosho (citrus mustard sauce), as needed
Soy Noodle Sauce (p 43. Or store-bought)

1 Remove seeds and pith from goya and slice into thin rounds.
2 Boil water in a pot. Run pork slices through boiling water (like shabu-shabu) until cooked then plunge into ice water, then place on strainer. Reserve boiling liquid.
3 In the same pot, blanch goya. Place on strainer.
4 In the same pot, boil vermicelli according to package directions. Drain.
5 Plate vermicelli, goya and pork (in that order). Top with grated daikon. Drizzle with Soy Noodle Sauce. Garnish with *shiso* and *yuzu kosho*.

Halve recipe to create small servings that are best for a post-drink bite.

Tomato & Black Sesame Vermicelli

The contrast between red and black makes a big impact. Add more sesame than you think you need.

Ingredients (serves 4)
4 servings vermicelli
5 plum tomatoes
    Pinch salt
5 Tbsp ground black sesame seeds
1 Tbsp vinegar
Myoga ginger buds, as needed
Salty Noodle Sauce (p 43), as needed

1 Roughly chop tomatoes and remove seeds. Add to bowl, dust with salt and let sit for 10 minutes. Drain off "sweated" liquid.
2 Add sesame and vinegar to tomatoes and mix. (There should be a lot of sesame.)
3 Boil vermicelli according to package instructions. Massage under running water.
4 Plate vermicelli. Add mixture from step 2. Garnish with minced ginger buds. Drizzle with Salty Noodle Sauce.

Note: Adding Salty Noodle Sauce to the ground black sesame seeds creates a whole new sauce, which is also great with other dishes like *natto* fermented soybeans.

Seasonal Nagasaki Noodles

Just use store-bought noodles! The toppings will show off what's in season.

Ingredients (serves 4)
- 4 servings (appx. 14 oz) fried or plate-style noodles
- 7 oz (200 g) pork loin, thinly sliced
- 2 1/2 Tbsp (10 g) dried shrimp
  - 3 Tbsp lukewarm water
- 2 bunches edible chrysanthemum (or *komatsuna*, or spinach, depending on the season)
- 1 pack shimeji (pioppini) mushrooms
- ● Seasonings
  - 1 1/3 Tbsp oyster sauce
  - 1 1/3 Tbsp mirin
  - 1 Tbsp vinegar
  - 2 Tbsp ground sesame seeds
- 2 tsp sesame oil
- ● Starch Paste
  - 1 Tbsp potato (or corn) starch
  - 1 Tbsp water

1 Reconstitute dried shrimp in lukewarm water for 30 minutes. Reserve the soaking liquid for later use.

2 Chop chrysanthemum into 1 1/2" pieces. Chop up any large mushrooms. Cut pork into 1" slices.

3 Heat sesame oil in a large frying pan or wok. Add pork and shrimp and stir-fry. Once 70% cooked, add mushrooms then chrysanthemum and stir-fry. Add shrimp soaking liquid and all seasonings and continue to stir-fry.

4 Pour in Starch Paste and stir until evenly distributed. Plate noodles and top with stir-fry.

Adventures in Seasonings!

Seasonings play a major role in simply prepared dishes. I often advise buying new kinds of seasonings over treating oneself to a new camisole. You might think some are on the pricey side, but you put food in your body every day, and cuisine that's brimming with love is delicious and fortifying. Here I'll introduce my favorite seasonings and staple ingredients. This is just for reference, so feel free to quest for your own favorites.

Soy Sauce (Dark and Light)

The gentle flavor of soy sauce goes great with all kinds of cuisine. Nagasaki soy sauce, from Kyushu, isn't sweet at all. Choose whatever type you like best, based on your preferences or style of cooking.

Mirin

Which one you use can significantly affect your cooking. Try tasting different kinds. There's one brand, Fuku Mirin, that's so rich I'd want to drink it on the rocks. The light-hued Yaezakura is mellower.

Vinegar

I use all kinds of Japanese rice vinegars, but I like the Saika brand if applying straight. The best bottles of vinegar are made with the same care that goes into sake brewing.

Miso (White and Red)

I was shocked when I first tried Yamari miso pastes in Kyoto. Such a natural sweetness! They're great eaten straight, that's how mellow they are. These misos are spoonable even when frozen, so I keep mine in the freezer and use them sparingly. If you ever go to Kyoto, look for some!

Canola and Egoma Oils

When a recipe lists "vegetable oil" this is generally what I use when frying. Flax seed oil is very similar to egoma (perilla) oil. Neither has much of a scent, so they're very useful in recipes where you don't want to add too much oily fragrance. Try using these in salad dressings, too.

Sesame Oil

The gentle fragrance and flavor of the Yamanaka brand goes great with any cuisine, East or West. I use them frequently in dressings, too.

Olive Oil

Monti del Duca (right) has the powerfully fresh flavor of green, grassy fields. It's wonderful with greens or just on bread. Olio Roi (left) is great with pasta and risotto, or with other rich foods. This oil is good even emulsified.

Dark Brown Sugar

I use superfine and brown sugar as well, but for richness and fragrance I tend to go for dark brown. It doesn't have the same direct sweetness of cane sugar, so if you want to really sweeten a dish, add a little extra.

Sake Lees (*sake kasu*)

I was surprised to see that these come in a tub. I was also surprised by how sumptuous the flavor is. It's soft and easy to use, which lets you expand your culinary horizons. You might want to eat it as-is!

Bonito Flakes (*katsuo bushi*)

Flakes that include the darker sections of bonito are still plenty tasty. I purchase them wholesale since they tend to be more reasonable that way.

Pink Peppercorns

I use these all the time when making meals for entertaining, since they immediately raise the level of whatever dish they're decorating. You can find these in any finer grocery store. They're hardly spicy at all. You can even put them on desserts.

Shaved Kelp (*tororo kombu*)

I prefer Gagome kelp, from Hokkaido. The sticky texture is a bit different, more wild. It's great just steeped in boiling water. Try using in rice balls or just mixed with dressing.

Tiny Rice Crackers (*bubu arare*)

These are so versatile they can be used as a topping for all kinds of dishes. Add to tea to boost cuteness. These make even rice porridge seem like a fancy treat.

Risotto Rice

Italian carnaroli rice, plump with very little stickiness, is ideal for risotto. It's almost pasta-like. Try mixing with Japanese white rice and enjoy the dual textures.

Short Pasta

Faella is the king of dried pasta. Cook al dente and you'll be able to appreciate how savory wheat really is. You can't go wrong with this one. Try searching online.

Brown Sugar Syrup / Crema di Balsamico / Raw Sugar Syrup

Try these on ice cream for a sophisticated dessert! Crema di Balsamico (center), or reduced balsamic vinegar, is so thick you could paint with it. Brown sugar syrup (left) and raw sugar syrup (right) go great with blue cheese.

part 6

Homemade Desserts: So Simple and Easy You'll Want to Congratulate Yourself!

You say making a dessert on top of everything else isn't easy? Hang in there to the end, you'll feel that much more satisfied and proud. It's important to feel like you accomplished something when you entertain guests.

These pleasing desserts are simple and can be made in a hurry or prepped ahead of time so you can be at ease when your guests are present. Don't worry about making precise measurements—this is a hit parade of fail-proof recipes.

Tiramisu

This is a recipe that
I learned from a Mamma in
Venice, no less. It might be
the most straightforward
one in the world.

Ingredients (serves 4 to 5)
- 2 1/2 Tbsp instant coffee
  - 1 C hot water
  - 2 Tbsp coffee liqueur or rum
- 15 ladyfingers (savoiardi)
- 3 egg yolks
- 1/3 C (70 g) granulated sugar
- 1 C (250 g) Mascarpone cheese
- Banana, soaked in rum for 30 minutes, as needed
- Coffee Jelly*, as needed
- Cocoa powder, as needed

1 Stir instant coffee into hot water.
Add liqueur and let cool.
2 Line serving dish with ladyfingers
and thoroughly coat with coffee.
3 Break up and stir egg yolks with a
spatula. Stir in sugar. Once thickened,
stir in Mascarpone cheese.
4 Pour cheese mixture onto
ladyfingers. Refrigerate for 2 to 3 hours.
5 Garnish with banana slices and
mashed coffee jelly. Dust with cocoa
powder.

Note: If bringing to a potluck, you can make
this the day before and freeze overnight.

Use any kind of soft, biscuit-like
cookies if you don't have ladyfingers.

*Coffee Jelly
(yields one 5" x 6" pan)

8 sheets (12 g) gelatin
1 2/3 C coffee
4 Tbsp dark brown sugar
1 Tbsp coffee liqueur or rum

1 Bloom gelatin in water for
about 15 minutes.
2 Heat coffee to about 170°F
(80°C). Add sugar, liqueur
and gelatin and dissolve
well. Pour into pan, let cool,
then refrigerate for about 3
hours or until solidified.
Note: The same coffee flavor
but a different texture adds
dimension.

Brown Sugar Jelly & *Yukari* Dumplings

Yukari is dried red *shiso*, often served on rice, but here it adds fragrance to dumplings. These are fun to make with friends!

Ingredients (serves 5 to 6)
- Brown Sugar Jelly
  - 1/2 C sake
  - 1 2/3 C water
  - 1/2 C (packed, 100 g) dark brown sugar
  - 10 sheets (15 g) gelatin
- *Yukari* Dumplings (yields about 15)
  - 2/3 C (100 g) *shiratama-ko* (glutinous rice flour)
  - 2 tsp *yukari shiso* seasoning
  - 1/2 C water
Poppy seeds, as needed

1 Make jelly: Bloom gelatin in water (extra) for about 10 minutes. Add sake, water and brown sugar to a pot and turn on heat. Turn off heat once gently boiling and add gelatin, mixing thoroughly.

2 Pour gelatin mixture into moistened pan and let cool. Refrigerate for 3 hours or until solidified.

3 Make dumplings: Add rice flour and *yukari* to a bowl and 80% of the water and knead. Add rest of the water as needed until the texture is slightly stiffer than an earlobe.

4 Roll dough into 1″ balls and create an indent in the middle of each. Boil for 6 to 7 minutes or until buoyant. Cool dumplings in water.

5 Plate dumplings and jelly. Garnish with poppy seeds.

Note 1: The dumplings are best when freshly boiled, but they can sit in water for 2 to 3 hours.
Note 2: You can use powdered agar (2 1/2 tsp; 6 g) instead of gelatin. Agar gels at room temperature, making it a good choice for a potluck dessert.

> **Gelatin vs. Agar**
> Gelatin solidifies when refrigerated, melts at room temperature and will not gel after being boiled. Agar solidifies at room temperature and doesn't melt, and must be stirred and heated thoroughly in order for it to be well incorporated into liquid. Use either gelatin or agar depending on the kind of dish you're preparing.

Ice Cream Sandwiches

These count as homemade no matter what anyone says!

Ingredients (serves 4)
5 1/4 oz (150 g) vanilla ice cream
8 cookies
20 raisins
   Rum, as needed

1 Soak raisins in rum for 30 minutes.

2 Drain raisins and stir into ice cream.

3 Sandwich ice cream between pairs of cookies. Wrap in plastic wrap and freeze for 2 hours or until solidified.

Note 1: Try using the Sour Cream & Marmalade or Sour Cream & Coffee dips between the cookies, too (recipes on p 10).
Note 2: These will keep frozen for up to 3 days.

Ice Cream di Balsamico

Just add Balsamico to transform plain ice cream into a ristorante-style treat. I might be brilliant.

Ingredients and Instructions

> Drizzle Crema di Balsamico (reduced balsamic vinegar) over ice cream.

Note: Try making with Brown Sugar Syrup or Raw Sugar Syrup (introduced on p 63). These syrups sure come in handy.

Dried Sweet Potato Parfait

This recipe is so special I almost don't want to share it. I gave it a fancy name because it's so challenging (?) to make.

Ingredients
16 oz (450 g) unsweetened yogurt
4 strips (appx. 3 oz) dried sweet potato
Raisins, dried cranberries, to taste

Making sure it doesn't overflow, pack in tight.

1 Chop sweet potatoes into 1" pieces.

2 Pack sweet potatoes into yogurt. Add raisins, dried cranberries or other fruits to taste.

3 Seal and refrigerate for at least half a day.

Note: The dried sweet potatoes will absorb moisture from the yogurt, giving them an unusual texture. This is a treat that's really hard to stop eating once you start!

All Red Jelly

This is made with red ingredients, yielding an adorable yet stylish and grown-up dessert.

Ingredients (serves 4 to 5)
- Red Jelly
  - 6 strawberries
  - 3 1/2 oz (100 g) blueberries
  - 1 tsp lemon juice
  - 6 sheets (9 g) gelatin
  - 1/2 C cassis liqueur, red wine or Kirsch
  - 1 C water
  - 2 Tbsp granulated sugar
- Red Sauce
  - 6 strawberries
  - 10 blueberries
  - 1 3/4 oz (50 g) raspberries
  - 1 Tbsp granulated sugar
  - 1 Tbsp cassis liqueur, red wine or Kirsch
  - 1 tsp lemon juice

1 Make jelly: Roughly chop strawberries and blueberries and drizzle with lemon juice. Bloom gelatin in water (extra).
2 In a pot, combine liqueur, water, sugar, strawberries and blueberries and turn on heat. Once gently boiling, turn off heat and add gelatin and stir until totally dissolved. Pour into dishes and let set up in the refrigerator for 3 hours.
3 Make sauce: Reserve 2 strawberries for garnish and slice the rest into eighths. Halve blueberries. Reserve 8 raspberries for garnish and add the rest to a pan, along with strawberries and blueberries. Add sugar, liqueur and lemon juice. Let sit for 15 minutes.
4 Set pan over low heat. Turn off heat once bubbling and let cool.
5 Pour sauce over jelly and garnish with sliced strawberries and raspberries.

Orange Jellies

These look tricky, but they're actually easy to make. They're a lovely way to celebrate the citrus season. Use agar, which stays gelled at room temperature, to bring over to friends.

Ingredients (yields 2 servings)
3 oranges
2 tsp (4 g) powdered agar
3 Tbsp honey
1 tsp lemon juice
Dash Cointreau

1 Slice 1/2" of one end of two oranges. Reserve cut off ends for use as lids.
2 Using a knife, carefully cut flesh away from the orange rinds, taking care to avoid cutting through. Squeeze flesh out of oranges.
3 Peel remaining orange and reserve 1/2 the flesh. Combine other 1/2 of flesh with flesh from the first 2 oranges. Wrap in cheesecloth and squeeze out juice (should yield 1 1/2 C).
4 In a pan, combine orange juice, honey, lemon juice, Cointreau and agar. Heat, stirring thoroughly. Once boiling, turn off heat and let cool.
5 Place reserved orange flesh inside the 2 orange rind cups and top off with orange jelly liquid. Let set up for 4 hours at room temperature. Serve chilled for best flavor.

Grown-Up Granita

Granita is a Sicilian specialty.

■ Watermelon Granita

Ingredients (for easy prep)
1 C (150 g) watermelon
1/2 C Campari
1/2 tsp sugar (superfine, brown or granulated)

> Dice watermelon, removing seeds. Place all ingredients in a mixer and blend. Pour into a baking dish and freeze for 1 1/2 hours. Remove from freezer, stir up with a fork, then freeze again. Repeat 2 to 3 times.

■ Basil Granita

Ingredients (for easy prep)
25 leaves fresh basil   1 tsp dark brown sugar
1/2 C Chartreuse liqueur   Lemon rind as garnish
2 Tbsp water

> Place all ingredients except lemon rind in a mixer and blend. Pour into a baking dish and freeze for 1 1/2 hours. Remove from freezer, stir up with a fork, then freeze again. Repeat 2 to 3 times. Garnish with lemon peel before serving.

Compote

A practical, everyday compote and an uncooked, raw food-style compote. Try substituting a variety of fruits.

■ Persimmon & Brown Sugar Compote

Ingredients (for easy prep)
2 persimmons   1/2 C sake (or vodka)
2 tsp lemon juice   2 Tbsp mirin (or sherry)
1/2 C dark brown sugar   Dash cinnamon powder

1 Peel persimmons, slice into sixths and remove seeds.
2 Line a pan with persimmons. Drizzle with lemon juice and dust with sugar. Let sit for 1 hour.
3 Add sake, mirin and cinnamon and simmer on low for 20 to 30 minutes. Turn off heat and let cool. Pour fruit along with liquid into a storage container and keep refrigerated until served.

■ Raw Fig (Heh!) Compote

Ingredients (for easy prep)
2 fresh figs
   1 pinch salt
1 Tbsp brown or granulated sugar
4 Tbsp red wine

1 Peel figs and quarter. Place figs in a strainer lined with paper towels, dust with salt and let sit for 30 minutes.
2 Wipe "sweat" from figs and place in a bowl. Add sugar and red wine and stir to coat. Refrigerate for 2 hours.

part 7

Coordinate Your Table Dressing to Suit the Occasion

Some say presentation is 70% of a meal's appeal. That's why I feel table dressing is a very important finishing touch. You can cover for any lack of confidence in your cooking skills this way. Try using a prominent color in the food as your main theme, or arrange seasonal flowers by the place settings. Think of the faces of your guests and have fun.

A Variety of Fun Table Dressings

Pair a bold red table runner with a beige tablecloth.
I like using cups with the same shape but in different patterns.

On the menu: Mexican. Skip the stereotypical red and yellow and go casual with a textured tablecloth and kitschy dishes instead.

Cool whites for summer. Try using real seashells for chopstick rests and shell-shaped dishes. Place a large frond under a glass dish for a refreshing centerpiece.

I coordinated the table dressing to match a gift of orange orchids which I also placed on plates. Try recipes with oranges on such a day.

An Early-Summer Ladies' Lunch

Put out a wide variety of foods at the start so you can spend your time chatting.

Menu

Serve right away:
- Figs & Blue Cheese (p 53)
- Beans & *Tsukudani* (p 53)
- Carrot Sandwiches, Cucumber Sandwiches (see right)
- Mango & Cranberry Salad (p 16)

Dishes that need a little prep:
- Onion Soup (p 48) + curry powder
- Grilled Broad Beans
- Goya Burgers (p 45)
- Dried Sweet Potato Parfait (p 67)

Notes:
▶ If you serve enough food at the beginning you won't need to always run to the kitchen, which helps keep the conversation going.
▶ This selection allows your guests to eat as much of what they like as they want, which makes the atmosphere more casual. This is also an approach that accommodates people who need to leave early or those whose preferences you don't know.

Steps

▶ Place sandwiches on a dampened cloth napkin or under parchment paper to keep from drying out.
▶ Choose a good time to heat up the soup before serving.
▶ Grill Goya Burgers ahead of time, cover with a lid and reheat briefly before serving.
▶ Place unpeeled broad beans under a broiler and cook for 6 to 7 minutes.
▶ Make dessert ahead of time and keep in refrigerator until serving.

Table Setting

▶ Coordinating with the colors of the sandwiches, salad and goya, choose yellow and green decorations.
▶ For the early-summer get-together, use dishes with fruit or seashell motifs that ladies will notice.

focus

Left: Serve pintxos individually for a cuter presentation. Right: Add 1 tsp curry powder to the recipe for Onion Soup (p. 48) for a curried twist.

Carrot Sandwiches, Cucumber Sandwiches

Familiar sandwiches, fresh arrangement. The fillings can be used to make salads, too.

Ingredients (serves 4)

Carrot Sandwiches
8 slices bread
2 carrots
  1 tsp salt
● Vinegar Raisins
  3 Tbsp raisins
  3 Tbsp vinegar
Mayonnaise, as needed

1 Soak raisins in vinegar for 2 hours (Vinegared Dried Fruits, p 16).
2 Grate carrots roughly (a fluffy texture allows them to absorb more of the dressing). Stir in salt and let sit for 20 minutes then press out liquid.
3 Pour vinegar and raisins over carrots and mix well. Let marinate for 1 hour.
4 Spread a thin layer of mayonnaise on bread and make 4 sandwiches with carrot filling. Stack 2 sandwiches together, place on a damp cloth napkin or wrap in parchment paper. Slice in half before plating.

Cucumber Sandwiches
8 slices bread
1 cucumber
  1 tsp salt
1 1/4 C (300 g) plain, unsweetened yogurt (drained*)
1 Tbsp lemon juice
4 slices cheese
* Line a strainer with paper towels and place yogurt inside. Let drain for half a day.

1 Peel stripes into cucumber and chop into thin, small pieces. Stir in salt and let sit for 20 minutes then press out liquid.
2 Stir yogurt and lemon juice into cucumbers.
3 Layer sliced cheese and cucumber mixture onto bread and make 4 sandwiches. Keep sandwiches from drying out and slice in half before plating.
Note: Try serving open-faced, too.

For When Your Mother-in-Law Drops By...

Keep things elegant yet effortless in order to impress the madam.

Menu

Serve right away:
- Pintxos (use chestnuts, ginko nuts, etc.)
- Chrysanthemum and Tangerine Salad (p 47)
- Pickles

Serve when the timing is right:
- Non-Stop *Jako* & Pine Nuts (p 18)
- Boiled Taro (see right), Fried Tofu Rolls (p 49) and Okra *Shioji Happo* (p 43)
- Yellowtail Dumplings (p 46)
- Dried Mackerel & Ginger Rice (p 58)
- Brown Sugar Jelly & *Yukari* Dumplings (p 66)

Notes:
▶ These dishes can be prepped ahead of time, allowing you to taste and check them so even Japanese cuisine won't be all that intimidating.
▶ These are reliably delicious, so use a modern presentation and watch as she calls you a seasoned chef.

Steps

▶ Make tofu rolls and okra the day before to let the flavors deepen.
▶ You can prep the tangerine ponzu and *jako* nuts up to 2 days in advance.
▶ You can cook the taros ahead of time. Marinate the tofu rolls in *dashi* broth, too.
▶ On the day of the meal, boil the chrysanthemum and make Yellowtail Dumplings (broth can be made in advance), Dried Mackerel & Ginger Rice and Brown Sugar Jelly & *Yukari* Dumplings.

Table Setting

▶ Arrange flowers on branches on Japanese-style dishes.
▶ Use Japanese lacquered boxes for foods for extra hosting points.
▶ Japanese cuisine can seem plain, so use larger dishes to stage a banquet.

focus

Top left: Use lacquered boxes if you can find them. Boxes with lids will keep food from drying out on the table.

Top right: A low-lying flower arrangement won't feel too imposing while still pulling everything on the table together. Here I used a Japanese food dish as a vase.

Left: Plate boiled ingredients in an elegant bowl for a different presentation.

Boiled Taro

Taro that's been thoroughly boiled in seasonings has a very mild flavor. These are great even cold.

Ingredients (serves 4)

8 taro (or yams)	1 Tbsp sugar
Dash salt	2 Tbsp mirin
Water, as needed	2 Tbsp light soy sauce
Pinch rice	1 tsp dark soy sauce (for fragrance)
1 1/4 C broth	

1 Peel taros and chop into bite-size pieces. If you have time, bevel sides.

2 Rub taros with salt, rinse, then place in pot with enough water to cover and add a pinch of rice. Boil until softened but still resistant when a skewer is inserted.

3 Make sure taros aren't overlapping. Add broth until submerged, cover with parchment paper and heat over medium-high for 5 to 6 minutes. Once boiling, turn heat to low, add sugar and simmer for 5 to 6 minutes. Add light soy sauce and mirin and simmer for another 25 minutes or until liquid has reduced to 1/3 volume.

4 Drizzle with dark soy sauce and let cool. Serve with tofu rolls and optionally garnish with *yuzu* peel.

Note: Cover with a parchment paper lid to force convection and keep taros from drying out.

A Casual yet Luxurious Christmas

Don't feel like you have to stick to traditional reds and greens!

Menu

Serve right away:
- 3 Dips (p 11, My Hummus, Sake Lees Blue Cheese, Miso Butter) + veggie sticks, crackers
- White Mushroom Salad (see right)
- Green Salad

Serve when the timing is right:
- Avocado Gratin (p 6)
- Whole Chicken Stew (p 40)
- Risotto (p 41)
- All Red Jelly (p 68)

Notes:
▶ Serve lots of side dishes from start to finish so you can bring everything out at your own pace.
▶ The main dish should be special enough that your guests cheer when it comes to the table.
▶ Keep the risotto for last, for those guests with heartier appetites, so you won't need to worry about anyone feeling underserved.

Steps

▶ Make the dips at least a day in advance.
▶ Prep Whole Chicken Stew ahead of time and reheat before serving.
▶ Dress White Mushroom Salad just as guests arrive.
▶ Place Avocado Gratin in the oven so it's ready to be broiled at any time.
▶ Start Risotto when you serve the Whole Chicken Stew.
▶ Make All Red Jelly in advance and keep refrigerated until serving.

Table Setting

▶ Go with an image that's slightly off the usual Christmas path.
▶ Use holiday cards in a casual way by writing the dinner menu or a message for your guests inside.
▶ Line the table with fun seasonal craft items.
▶ Decorate your everyday plates with red ribbons to make them feel festive.

focus

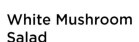

Top left: Even the All Red Jelly is red, like the decor.
Top right: Your regular dishes can also work in a holiday theme. Tie up napkins with red and navy ribbons and string.
Center left: I bought this tablecloth at Ikea. This inspired me to tie everything together with reds.
Center right: Write the menu on holiday cards. Try using foreign-language newspapers as tablecloth.
Bottom left: Simple red string transforms basic serving dishes.
Bottom right: Upgrade your usual glasses simply by placing them on a plate.

White Mushroom Salad

Feel free to use large mushrooms. Your guests will be addicted from the first bite.

Ingredients (serves 4)

15 white mushrooms	2/3 C white miso
1 C sour cream	2 tsp lemon juice

1 Combine sour cream, miso and lemon juice and stir well.
2 Remove stems and dirt from mushrooms. Slice in half lengthwise and add to a bowl.
3 Combine right before serving, thoroughly coating mushrooms with sour cream dressing.

This was for a Christmas gathering. I used a grown-up pink theme with different shades of pink plus white.

In small glasses, a flower per person. There's a wide variety of pink flowers, so your guests can choose their favorite.

Peonies dress up otherwise plain-looking cuisine. I found those napkin rings in Thailand.

White is a common color I use for first-time guests. Rattan placemats and carefree flowers ease any tension.

Afterword

310 West 52nd Street. That was the address I shared with my husband when we lived in New York City in 2007. We only lived there for just over a year, but it was during this time that I began to pray that I could live the rest of my life working in the food industry. Actually, I reverted to a child-like wish to spend my life doing what I wanted, and I discovered that I wanted to work with food.

In New York I met an aspiring stand-up comedian, Rio. You're probably familiar with the type of tiny, plain comedy clubs that dot the city where the stage is just a few feet from the audience. As the audience members sit there, drink in hand, the performers show off their skills in this spoken-word craft, using anecdotes about culture and regionalisms alone on the stage, occasionally infuriating those they attempt to entertain. It's a lonely and potentially dangerous job. Rio earned $20 per gig. He shared an apartment with a man from India and worked part-time to make ends meet.

Even with such a lifestyle, he seemed happy. I always wondered why. Wasn't he anxious about the future? Weren't there things he wanted? We met when I was managing a small company where I had begun accepting jobs that I didn't love just for the money. Meeting him made me think deeply, reevaluating what I considered to be happiness.

Coming into contact with countless others like him, I had decided by the time I went back to Japan to reset my life and set out on the path I'd abandoned, the one where I share my love of cooking with people I care about.

As that idea took root and grew, I cooked and ate across the city to my heart's content. From the start of my stay I chose to never go to Japanese grocery stores, preferring to only buy food in places like green markets, Whole Foods and Zabar's. Even so, I was able to make all kinds of cuisine, from Japanese to European to Chinese, even fusion foods. The great thing about Japanese home-style cooking is the ability to incorporate Asian or Western-style cuisine into everyday meals.

There are plenty of recipes in this book that were created during that time which turned into household hits. For example, my comedian friend's favorite dish was the Mexican-inspired coffee-infused roast pork, which is why I named it "Manhattan-Style." I would always cook up two pounds of pork so there would be enough for leftovers. That recipe brings back memories.

At the time, I also took cooking classes. The one that made the biggest impression was De Gustibus Cooking School. De Gustibus has guest teachers come from across the country and teach the students directly. I was able to study under such greats as Chef Gabriel Kreuther of my favorite restaurant The Modern and the very popular Rachael Ray. I learned a great deal.

What's more, a miracle happened and a dream came true when I was somehow able to meet David Bouley. He left a major impression on me. I'll never forget sharing food in his amazing test kitchen, seeing his new restaurant (then still under construction) and hearing him talk passionately about his deep knowledge of Japanese cuisine.

I would also like to thank the New Yorkers who always came over to enjoy my cooking, praising my efforts. Matthew, Yasmin, Saito, Chika & Rio, thank you from the bottom of my heart.

It sounds dramatic, but I'm very moved that my book is being printed in English by a publisher based in New York City, the city that changed my life. This book is filled with recipes that I made while in America and I'm sure you'll be able to recreate them easily. It would please me more than anything if you'd think of your family and loved ones and enjoy the process of making food as you cook up these recipes. Lastly—dedicated with love to my beloved husband.

Riko Yamawaki

Riko Yamawaki
Presides over "Riko's Kitchen." Food coordinator,
nutrition instructor. Born in an old tourist ryokan in
Nagasaki, Ms. Yamawaki loves seasonal ingredients,
dishes and arrangements. Aside from traveling the world
sampling markets and restaurants and learning how to
prepare local foods, she studied French cuisine at ADF
(Alain Ducasse Formation + Conseil). Her mother was her
first cooking teacher. As Ms. Yamawaki's love of
entertaining burgeoned, she opened a food salon at
home with her friends in 2005 while working for a PR
consulting firm.
In 2010, she opened a small culinary class in Daikanyama,
Tokyo, called "Riko's Kitchen." Her lessons on in-season
ingredients, stylings to suit the time of year and preparing
dashi grew popular. She spent one year starting in 2007
in New York and now lives with her husband in Tokyo.

Blog: ameblo.jp/marukinsyokudo
Facebook: facebook.com/Rikoskitchen
Riko's Kitchen Cooking Class: marukin.exblog.jp

Photography/Styling: Riko Yamawaki
Book Design: Ryo Takahashi
Planning/Composition: Maiko Shimizu

Banzai Banquets
Party Dishes that Pack a Punch

Translation: Maya Rosewood
Vetter: Maria Hostage
Production: Hiroko Mizuno
          Grace Lu

Motenashigohan No Netacho
© 2011 Riko Yamawaki. All rights reserved.
First published in Japanese as *Motenashi Go-han no Neta-cho* in 2011
by Kodansha Ltd., Tokyo.
English edition rights arranged through Kodansha Ltd.

Translation provided by Vertical, Inc., 2013
Published by Vertical, Inc., New York

ISBN: 978-1-935654-92-6

Manufactured in the U.S.A.

First Edition

Vertical, Inc.
451 Park Avenue South, 7th Floor
New York, NY 10016
www.vertical-inc.com